VIKKI L. PENDLETON

BECOMING A WEALTHY BELIEVER

The Believer's Keys To Success

Contents

Introduction

Dear Chosen,

Hopefully this will be a short and to the point introduction of my first book. It's been a long time coming because I had to learn so much and it took years of many experiences to grow into.

My legal name is Vikki LeTonya Pendleton. My nickname is Sugar. I am a Christian Hip Hop artist and Christian stage DJ for concerts and Christian events that have performers. Please listen to my music on any listening format. You can find it under my artist's name DJ JChill or DJ JCHILL. (Some formats are case sensitive).

JCHILL is an acronym for Jesus Christ Has Infinite Lasting Love.

Once this book hits the market, I will be offering services for Power Couple Contracts, Matrimony Contracts, Consultations to help you find your Divine Purpose, Consultations on developing into becoming a Chosen vessel, specifically tailored Daily Affirmations for you, Speaking engagements, conferences, conventions, book signings, music performances, concerts, and Stage DJ formats.

The purpose of this book is to explain to God's Chosen vessels how to create and maintain a successful and wealthy lifestyle by using key strategies in the Bible for walking in your Divine purpose. Often times throughout the book I will make reference to a "key" which is noting an important point for wealth building.

All Characters are fictitious unless otherwise stated for the purpose of illustrating my point or an example.

Certain things are repeated consistently throughout the Bible. In my book I also repeat certain things consistently. The purpose of this repetition within the Bible is the same purpose for the repetition in this book, it is because it is of strong importance and most people ignore this particular important thing that I am writing on in that passage. The more you hear it, the more apt you will be to grasp it. Therefore, I repeat it, and I give repeated different scenarios hoping that the Chosen vessel will understand the importance and adopt the certain characteristic that I am repeating because it is a must that it be mastered by the Chosen.

Becoming A Wealthy Believer is a trilogy. All three books should be studied and mastered by all who resonate with it.

Thank you to you that believed in me, you know who you are. And thank you to you that didn't, you know who you are as well. I am Vikki the Victorious Victor, I guess you didn't know the meaning of my name.

With All My Love,

Vikki aka Sugar aka DJ JCHILL

1

CHAPTER 1

WHAT DOES THE BIBLE SAY ABOUT WEALTH?

When I think about what the Bible says about wealth, the first thing that comes to mind is that wealth is not just money. Wealth is made up of so many more elements than just financial gain. Wealth for the believer is wisdom and knowledge, power through the Holy Spirit, peace, safety, joy, Divine provision, as well as financial and material gain.

When we think of wealth, we think of what we can do with money. To many people wealth is a great paying job or business, being debt free, having lots of material assets, and a bank full of money. But the Bible does not promise us any of those things.

In the Bible we have illustrations of God's faithful believers being rich as well as poor. King Jehoshaphat, the son of David, had riches and honor in abundance. 1Chronicles 17:5. In the book of Job we learn that Job had been rich, then poor, and then even richer than the first time mentioned. Mathew 27:57 tells us of a disciple of Jesus named Joseph who was a rich man. Mark 12:42 speaks of the poor widow that gave 2 coins very small in value yet was more than all the others put together. Proverbs 22:2 proclaims, "The rich and the poor have this in common, the Lord is the maker of them all."

Believers come from all walks of life. Some believers are rich, some poor, and others middle class. Some believers are in debt up to their ears, while other believers may be debt free. There are even homeless believers! Our financial circumstance does not make us greater or lesser in the eyes of God. Just because a believer is monetarily rich does not mean that God loves him more than the poor believer. He loves us all the same. "For there is no partiality with God." Romans 2:11.

We all will be judged accordingly by God. The wonderful news is that as a believer in Christ, we can have all the elements of wealth on Earth and in the end, we will have eternal life in a place we call Heaven. Which is the ultimate element of wealth!

While we are here on this Earth, why not have wealth in abundance? I'm certain that all people want wealth, but not all people can handle or possess great wealth. For some people money runs through their hands like water. For other people great wealth is unattainable. Some people don't know what to do with it when they have it, and others just can't figure out how to get it. That's where this book comes in. If you follow these keys to success, mapped out for God's Chosen few, you should be well on your way to Becoming a Wealthy Believer!

2

CHAPTER 2

7 BIBLICAL ELEMENTS OF WEALTH

- Wisdom and Knowledge
- Power Through His Holy Spirit
- Peace
- Safety
- Joy
- Divine Provision
- Financial and Material Gain

Wisdom and Knowledge

A lot of people may think of wisdom and knowledge as the same thing. Some people believe you cannot have one without the other. This is very false. Wisdom and knowledge are not the same. They are very different, and you can have knowledge without having wisdom. The element of *complete* wealth in this area is, however, obtaining both wisdom and knowledge.

Wisdom is the quality of possessing experience, good judgement, obedience, understanding, and knowledge. Having insight into life and knowing the correct ways of dealing with what life throws your way is wisdom. A wise person is one that represents himself in a way that is respectable, orderly, obedient, caring, and compassionate, one that thinks before he speaks. A wise person is generally found to be a morally upright person.

Knowledge is knowing facts, information, having a skill or trade through education, experience, reading, or association. Knowledge is knowing things however you came to know it.

You can have knowledge and not possess wisdom. But to have wisdom includes having knowledge.

A police officer must be taught how to use his weapon. The police officer knowing how to use his weapon is knowledge. But a wise police officer knows the appropriate time to use his weapon, this is wisdom. Knowledge is knowing _how_ to use the weapon and wisdom is knowing _when_ to use the weapon that you have the knowledge of using.

-Using Wisdom

Many people have knowledge and lack wisdom. Think about a pastor who has a very successful church and ministry, but he has been married 3 times and divorced 3 times. He enjoys the company of women who are not his wife and entertains drug use with them. He knows the Bible, he knows how to teach and preach the Word of God, but he does not know how to apply this knowledge to his own personal life. He can quote the scriptures on how a husband should be towards his wife, but he lacks the wisdom to be obedient to that knowledge of the scripture. Instead, he suffers from and actively practices his addictions such as sexual immorality and drug use.

Knowledge memorizes the commandments and Word of God; wisdom obeys them.

There are many people who have Doctorate degrees and much schooling, yet they lack the wisdom to maintain a successful private life, marriage, and family. There are people that are very knowledgeable in vast areas of life, but make poor financial decisions, poor moral decisions, some cannot keep jobs, and many are living a very poor lifestyle. We see them and wonder, with all the smarts and knowledge they have, why would they not make wise decisions in their lives? This is simply because knowledge and wisdom are two very different things. Just because you have knowledge does not mean you automatically have wisdom.

The Bible clearly tells us in James 1:5, "If any of you lacks wisdom, he should ask God, who gives generously to all without finding fault, and it will be given to him." So, why are so many Christians lacking wisdom if all they must do is ask God?

Many Christians do not read the Word of God, do not fellowship with other Christians, and do not obey the Word of God. Reading the Bible is the Christians source to obtaining Wisdom and Knowledge. The Bible is your key to a successful life. The answers to all of life's questions and problems are in the Bible. It is important to be able to make wise decisions in your life, especially during difficult situations. You are going to have trials and tribulations in your life but if you lack the wisdom needed to overcome adversity, you will just keep making the same mistakes and you will never get ahead in life that way.

In 1 Kings 3:1-15, Solomon humbly prayed to God for wisdom and knowledge. Solomon, the son of King David, was now a king himself. He was not puffed up in his prayer, nor was he self-centered. Being of his statue he could very well have been "big headed" and "full of himself". I am sure we all know people like that, they have a position on a job or some type of social or governing position and it goes to their head, and they are very puffed up and self-centered. They have knowledge of their position but lack the wisdom needed to apply understanding and compassion for others that they lead, work with, or know.

l believe Solomon was humble when he prayed to God, he stated that "he was like a little child, and he did not know how to go out or come in." He went on to say he understood that he was in the midst of God's people and chosen by God.

When he said he was like a little child, he was saying he did not have the wisdom and experience to lead these people. And when he said he did not know how to go out or come in, he was saying he didn't know where to start or finish with leading God's chosen people. Before he prayed this prayer, he showed that he had been taught how to be a God-fearing man from watching his father, David. He told God, his father walked in faithfulness, righteousness, and uprightness of heart with You (God), and in return God showed David great mercy and loving kindness and made David's son King as well. Solomon did not pray for riches or money; he asked God for an understanding mind and a hearing heart to judge God's people. This is Humility. He was not self-centered, he was God-centered. He also recognized and knew the true source of Wisdom and Knowledge.

In return, God said to Solomon because he did not ask for long life, riches, or selfish desires, but instead asked for understanding to recognize what is just and right, He gave Solomon what he asked. He gave him a wise, discerning mind, so that no one before or after him could compare. God also gave him both riches and honor even though Solomon did not ask for that. God went on to tell Solomon that if he will go God's way, keep God's statues, and His commandments as did his father David, He will lengthen his days on Earth.

When we have our mind set on our own selfish desires, it holds us back from obtaining true wealth. What we see with Solomon's story is that wisdom is really being obedient to God, and the consequences of being obedient are the blessings of the Lord. As king, Solomon was to govern God's people, and he wanted to do a great job in his position as King. In this story we learn that being obedient to God, leads to living a righteous life. Using wisdom with the knowledge that you have leads to a longer life. We must know and apply God's word to have wisdom and knowledge. This is an element of being wealthy, full of wisdom and full of knowledge. In return you get a longer life and earthly riches.

Pray and ask God for wisdom and knowledge. Then read and study the Word of God and seriously apply it to your life. You will gain knowledge over time as you study the scriptures. You will gain wisdom as you learn how to apply this knowledge to applicable situations. Consciously live a righteous and morally upright life. You will be amazed at how intelligent and wise you will become and how the blessings will begin to flow into your life.

Step away from so much technology. Turn off the TV. Put down the cell phone. Get off the internet. These things create diversions from the art of true learning. I find that through these devices we absorb what the world wants us to know and believe. We need to absorb what the Heavenly Father wants us to know and believe and we cannot do that through a loud, chaotic source. Step into the natural creations of God and be still and quiet and allow the Holy Spirit to speak to you and teach you at that place. When a child of God has shared with you that he went to the mountain top and he met God there, understand that God is sending you a message of where to go so He can speak to you. Sit alone at the beach, or the riverside, in the hills and slopes of the land. Find solace in the splatter of natural waterfalls, the beauty of God's creations. Look for a place that is peaceful and only nature is the sound you hear. It is in this quiet place that the Holy Spirit will open your soul and pour into you what God wants you to know.

Power Through the Holy Spirit

One of the ways God will speak to you is through the Holy Spirit. The Holy Spirit dwells within you. God speaks to the Holy Spirit that is inside of you and the Holy Spirit transmits what God is saying to you from within. The Bible tells us that the Holy Spirit is our Teacher and will guide us through life. In John 14:26 Jesus says, "But the Helper, the Holy Spirit, whom the Father will send in My name, He will teach you all things and bring to your remembrance all things that I said to you". The Holy Spirit is more than just our Teacher, He guides us through life as our Comforter, Advocate, Counselor, Intercessor, Strengthener and He is always with us, and on standby at all times as He guides us through life's journey.

Those goals, dreams, and visions that have been in our hearts and on our minds for years, months, weeks, decades, are the things God has placed in us and has been translated to us as God's will for our lives through the Holy Spirit. It is not just our own creative mind but rather us implementing the creative will of God in our lives. The purpose of your life is to fulfill the will of God. It's why you were created. The Holy Spirit teaches us and guides us towards those things which God has chosen us to do.

This verse also tells us that the Holy Spirit will not let us forget that which God has created us to do. He will bring it to our remembrance when we need to use that knowledge. This can pertain to the use of Biblical scriptures as well as life's lessons. We can find ourselves in a situation where someone needs to be ministered to, and the Holy Spirit will bring to our remembrance the appropriate scripture. This even applies to our very own daily life. As we go through different situations the Holy Spirit will remind us of a scripture that will help us through that situation. To know the scripture, you must spend quality time studying the Word of God.

Life teaches us lessons as well. We should gain knowledge from everyday life. We have school that we must attend from a small child that teaches us the necessities needed for a future diploma. We go through life experiencing trials and tribulations, defeats, wins, highs, and lows, and we should learn something from each and every experience that we encounter. One day we will need that knowledge and wisdom that we have acquired and learned. At that time the Holy Spirit will bring it to our remembrance. Often times this may be our personal testimony, and other times it may just be the Holy Spirit directing us to use prior knowledge and growth from a previous situation.

Your dreams, goals, and visions that have been placed inside of you are the fruit that you will produce. As a believer we should yield to and obey God's Word and follow the path God has laid before us. When doing this we are living in the power of the Holy Spirit. We are allowing and relying on the Holy Spirit to guide us towards our destiny.

The Holy Spirit comes with 7 gifts. Those gifts are wisdom, understanding, counsel, fortitude, knowledge, piety, and the fear of the Lord. Through these 7 gifts of the Holy Spirit, we obtain power. We need this power to produce the fruits of our labor.

Wisdom is the first and greatest gift of the Holy Spirit. The Holy Spirit allows us to use wisdom to exert the will of God, and to wisely execute our own will in situations that we face in life. James 1:5 tells us "If any of you lacks wisdom, let him ask of God, who gives to all liberally and without reproach, and it will be given to him".

I cannot stress the importance of being able to make wise decisions in stressful and difficult situations. We as Christians can ask God for wisdom in any given situation and the Word tells us He will give us that without hesitation or disapproval. Generously, He will give us the wisdom we need just by asking for it. It is a shame to say, but many do not ask God for wisdom and make costly mistakes and live with regrets of making the wrong decision in difficult and stressful instances, as well as business decisions. Even in marriage and in divorce. If we would just yield to the power of the Holy Spirit and ask for guidance, we can avoid many stresses we cause on ourselves when we operate in our own power. When our responses and goals are self-centered and not God centered, we fail in obtaining the power of the Holy Spirit and the outcome usually is devastating to some degree.

When we say that we fear God, we are saying that we submit to His authority and His position as the God Head in our lives. Out of that respect we must take certain precautions and live our lives in a godly manner. We have the power to do this through His Holy Spirit. Failure to do so will prolong us reaching our goals.

Peace

Peace, peace, peace, peace. We all say we want peace, but do we really know what peace is? We view peace as having the absence of conflict and turmoil in our lives. No one "getting on our nerves" and disturbing our *peace.* We always see peace as a place of love and harmony, a quiet and calm moment of existence. The Bible tells us that this world is full of tribulations and as we go through life, we will experience many up-hill battles. Where is the peace in that?

I will tell you, peace is that feeling you have within you, when what is outside of you looks like chaos. But yet, you have *Peace in the midst of the storm.* No matter how bad the situation looks to you, you have this knowing that everything will be alright and will work in your favor. You are cool, calm, and collected with a confidence that is still and quiet while all hell has broken out in your life. That is peace.

The Bible tells us of a story where Jesus calms the storm by calling in "peace" and telling the storm to "be still". The disciples and Jesus had gotten on a boat and other little boats were with Him. A great wind and storm arose, maybe like a high category hurricane, and the waves of water were hitting against the boats and filling them with water. Jesus was asleep through this storm and the disciples woke him up asking him if he even cares that the boats are filling with water and could possibly sink and drown them all with it. Jesus got up and rebuke the wind, commanded peace, and told the sea to be still. Immediately the wind ceased and there was a great calm. Jesus then turned to the disciples and asked them why were they so fearful, and how is it that they have no faith?

This was a physical storm, but we experience storms in our lives in other forms of tribulation. These storms cause us anxiety, depression, anger, fear, and panic. None of which produces peace in our lives. Instead, it produces discord and unpleasant emotions leaving us faithless in the given situation. Not only does the negative way we react to the storms in our lives affect us, but it affects our loved ones and those around us negatively as well. The Bible mentioned that there were other smaller boats with them that had people on them. I am sure the panic of the disciples caused panic in everyone else that was with them, especially in the smaller boats because those boats were likely to sink first. Panic alone can cause negative results. They could have panicked to the point of falling out the boat and drowning or fighting amongst one another to get to the larger boat that Jesus was on to try to avoid drowning. Much like when we have a peaceful protest that turns into an ugly riot and it is no longer peaceful, and people began to get hurt and even killed. Everybody involved is in an uproar and there is no peace to be found, only a raging storm.

When we have no peace in our lives, we tend to have bad behaviors. We are not pleasant to be around because we are in a miserable place in our lives when peace is not present. Addictive behaviors can form to try to cope with the heaviness of the storm we are experiencing. You cannot achieve your greatest wealth with addictions. Addictions are expensive, eat up your wealth and will cause you to act carelessly in life. When you are looking for an advancement, (because we all need the assistance and help of someone else to get to where we are going), no one is going to trust an addict, or someone with a bad attitude, with an advancement of any kind. These are just irresponsible behaviors and a deterrent towards greatness. I strongly encourage anyone struggling with addiction of any kind to get help and overcome your addiction. Also, it is not shameful or embarrassing to seek out professional help for emotional issues. In fact, it is a necessity. If you do not receive the proper help and assistance for addictions and emotional issues, you are hindering your building blocks for obtaining wealth.

It is important to be a peaceful person by nature because God will not bless you with what you can't handle and what you do have you may lose. Wealth cannot be built when peace is not present. When you are calm, you can produce positive solutions to solve the issues causing the storm.

A wise ruler is not one that is prone to anxiety, panic, addictions, anger, and depression. A wise ruler calls in the Spirit of Peace and tells the storm to cease and "be still". Through faith, rebuke the storm and trust God for your favorable results.

When the disciples got into the boat, they had no idea a storm was coming. We must master having an inner peace during adversity because we do not know when an adverse situation will arise. If we did, we could prepare a strategy to defeat it and we would not be shocked when it hits us. Trials come from every direction and without warning. A lot of the initial negative responses to adversity are a result of the shock of the situation and being caught off guard. When you have mastered having peace in your life, no matter the situation or what life throws your way, your judgement will be clear, and you can persevere in all your endeavors.

Safety

Most people do not realize safety is an important key to reaching one's goals. Wikipedia says safety is the state of being "safe", the condition of being protected from harm or other non-desirable outcomes. Safety can also refer to the control of recognized hazards to achieve an acceptable level of risk.

Recently we had a Coronavirus Pandemic that we nicknamed COVID-19.

This disease is so fiercely devastating that it affected the entire planet! Life as we had known it immediately changed. We had to wear face masks in public and social distance at least 6 feet from one another. It shut down businesses, closed schools, ceased traveling and vacations, caused great illnesses, caused deaths, and unemployment reached an all-time high. Many people understood the severity of the disease and stayed inside their homes without socializing during the pandemic. Then there were the select few who didn't take it seriously and didn't wear face masks or try to adhere to the rules set in place to make it through the pandemic with the least number of deaths and illnesses as possible. Not everyone who did not take the pandemic seriously became affected and not everyone who did take the pandemic seriously escaped the grips of COVID-19. But the wise response was to be SAFE.

Doing unsafe things will eventually produce unsafe results and someone will get hurt. Being unsafe and not taking the necessary precautions during the Coronavirus Pandemic could result in grave illness and/or death of someone who became infected. It is our own individual responsibility to protect ourselves from injury, hurt, and loss. We limit our ability to create, learn, and teach when we are injured or hurt. Accidents happen, but when it is due to our own negligence and carelessness that is irresponsibility on our part. Being safe is being smart. Safety is a key element in wealth building.

Joy

Let us look at a story of an older lady that is mean and miserable. She is always sad and unhappy. She plays on these emotions in such a way to get attention from her children and family members. They are always catering to her whimpers and cries. When asked why she is so sad, she would say she does not have a happy life. Then it is pointed out to her all the people and family members that love her and do for her, and she acknowledges that she loves them too, but she is still unhappy. Someone then reads to her the scripture Nehemiah 8:10, "...Do not sorrow because the Joy of the Lord is your strength." And explained to her the keys to having real Joy and she would no longer feel sad and unhappy all the time. She has no comment because she does not want to change. She continues the rest of her life being a mean, sad, grumpy old lady. End of story.

One must realize, there are a lot of people who are comfortable being sad and miserable and want to stay that way.

What is the difference between Joy and happiness? Happiness is an emotion, and Joy is one of the fruits of the Spirit. Happiness is triggered by things, events, people, and moments that are external. Joy is sustained internally and is felt from within on a consistent basis. Let me explain.

Emotions are tied to our Earthly or Human nature. Happiness is an emotion that we experience while here on Earth. I homeschooled my children. Each child was homeschooled a different number of years before going to public school according to the need of the child. Each one of my children is doing well in life and are self-sufficient. My youngest graduated from high school and college with Honors. I was so happy to see my kids graduate from high school and then from college. Such a proud mom I am! The very thought makes me happy and smile. At any given moment one of those very same adult children can call me and say or do something I totally disagree with and that "happy proud mom" I was feeling will be instantly gone. I am sure all proud parents can understand that illustration of happiness and how quickly it can fade into a different emotion.

There was one time my family successfully surprised me with a birthday party. I am not easy to surprise, and they actually pulled it off. I was so happy the entire week. Here is a secret: The thought of melting marshmallows and making s'mores makes me happy. Going on vacations and exploring new places makes me happy.

I have a memory that makes me smile when I think of it, and I doubt I will ever forget it. One day as a child my mother was correcting a bad behavior that I displayed as we were going into the grocery store. At that moment I wasn't having good thoughts about her because she was reprimanding me, and I didn't like it. As we walked through the entry door of the store my mom tripped on the threshold and I burst out in laughter, glad that something seemingly embarrassing happened to her because she was embarrassing me at that moment. I will never forget that feeling of satisfaction and happiness I had at that moment when she tripped. It was quickly wiped away as she turned and hit me right upside my head knocking me into the oranges in the produce section! Oranges went everywhere as did my happy feeling. Happiness can possess the quality of being good or bad. I was clearly misbehaving and mischievous, being happy that something embarrassing happened to my mom.

We as humans partake in sinful things that give us pleasure and momentary happiness that are terrible things to do. In Galatians 5:19-21 it tells us what the works of the flesh are. Many are fleshy desires that bring us momentary happiness when we do them. Such as adultery, fornication, selfish ambitions, drunkenness, and things of the like. And we can experience happiness while entertaining our sinful nature although the act itself is bad.

Joy, on the other hand, is always a component of good. Joy is not momentary; it is consistent in its nature. Joy is not an emotion at all, it is one of the fruits of the Spirit. The Holy Spirit dwells inside of us and that is where Joy is found, within us. There is no person, event, or thing on Earth that can give us Joy. Joy is spiritual and it is given to us through the Holy Spirit. *To have Joy requires us to be Divinely connected to God.* Since the Holy Spirit dwells in us regardless of the circumstances or events taking place in our life, Joy is also able to be felt regardless of the circumstances or events taking place in our life. As we grow in our relationship with God so does the fruits of the spirit within us. We express our Joy when we worship, when we share testimonies, when we examine all that God has blessed us with in this life. When we think of all the trials, tribulations, and hardships God has brought us through, we feel this Joy from within. We can be in a prison cell and be full of Joy. Some of us have been through so much hell in this life, yet we are filled with so much Joy. And those of us can say, Hallelujah, I thank you Lord for this untouchable Joy!

John 16:24 NKJV Jesus says, "Until now you have asked nothing in My name. Ask, and you will receive, that your joy may be full." Until we have walked in our destiny, walked in that very thing God has created us to do, we are not full. Once we have done that, we will experience Joy at its fullness.

Divine Provision

Gloria: Mason, what church do you attend?

Mason: Although I was raised in church, as an adult I do not go to church or pray. It is not my lifestyle.

Gloria: Really? I never would have thought that of you because you have a six-figure job and are doing so well with your career.

Mason: That has nothing to do with going to church or praying to God.

Gloria: Why would you think that? You are so blessed and if you were raised in church then you know God hears your prayers, right?

Mason: No, He never heard my prayers, and I never heard Him speak to me. Everything I got, *I got it myself*, my efforts, my blood, sweat, and tears. It had nothing to do with God.

Gloria: Well then someone must be really praying for you because I see the hand of God on your life providing for you.

God is our provider. He supplies everything that we need. Psalm 37:25 says, "I have been young, and now am old; yet have I not seen the righteous forsaken, nor his seed begging bread."

It is through God's Divine Provision that all our needs are met in every aspect of our lives. We can live a physically and mentally healthy lifestyle and enjoy healthy relationships just by applying what we have learned in God's Word and by studying and reading material written for our benefit. We can achieve financial goals and live a life full of blessings in an abundance through the Divine Provision of God. "And you shall remember the Lord your God, for it is He who gives you power to get wealth, that He may establish His covenant which He swore to your fathers, as it is this day." Deuteronomy 8:18.

Many people take credit for their prosperity and success, as Mason did in the conversation above. They feel their very own planning, smarts, and hard work landed them in the high position they currently sit. The dangerous thing about that is they could lose everything they have once Grace and Mercy run out. There is nothing more important and valuable in this life than our relationship with God. No one on this planet can bless us more than God. In fact, it is God who uses others to be a blessing to us. The Bible tells us that all blessings come from the Lord. God is a good God; He is not a man that He should lie, and He keeps his promises to our forefathers. Our parents and grandparents sustain us with their prayers, and we are blessed, guided, and protected even when we are astray. It is not a wise thought to think that you have built your empire in the absence of God.

The Bible clearly tells us how to create wealth and enjoy a life full of abundance. Aside from being obedient to God's Word and will for your life, another step towards your greatness is to be a giver. *Give,* and it will be given to you. Just that plain and simple. If you give little, you get little. If you give a lot, you get a lot. When you give, do it out of the kindness of your heart and you will get back so much more.

People need our compassion, our humility, our loving kindness. People need to know and feel that we care about them. This is truly a blessed soul that gives this way to mankind. So many people are hurting and suffering in their lives, and we are placed directly in their lives for the purpose of giving them the tools that God has equipped us with to give. I cannot leave this Earth without writing this book. God has placed this book on my heart and other writings since I was 12 years old to give to the world. I cannot turn down a person that cries to me for help of some kind because I know God sent them to me so I can give to them what they need. Which means God already has given to me what it is that I need to give to them. Afterwards, God will miraculously multiply my blessing from what I have given and return it to me in the form that I need at that time. And He will do the same for you.

Selfishness is not a Godly thing. Selfishness is a hinderance in our daily lives and walk with God. We must learn to give to increase.

"Remember this: Whoever sows sparingly will also reap sparingly, and whoever sows generously will also reap generously. Each of you should give what you have decided in your heart to give, not reluctantly or under compulsion, for God loves a cheerful giver. And God is able to bless you abundantly, so that in all things at all times, having all that you need, you will abound in every good work. As it is written: "They have freely scattered their gifts to the poor, their righteousness endures forever." Now he who supplies seed to the Sower and bread for food will also supply and increase your store of seed and will enlarge the harvest of your righteousness. You will be enriched in every way so that you can be generous on every occasion, and through us your generosity will result in thanksgiving to God." 2Corinthians 9:6-11.

Give in faith knowing that God makes Divine Provision for you and will continue to do so. Work on increasing your faith within the area of giving so you don't hold back on giving generously. It is not too much that is free in this world, but a relationship with God is totally free. If we plan to build Kingdom wealth, we need a relationship with the King. He hears our prayers, and He speaks to us if we would listen.

Financial and Material Gain

Financial and material gain is the number one way that people measure wealth. Most people do not even see the other elements previously mentioned as components of wealth. You can go on the internet and look up the net worth of any famous person and it is available for the world to see. It is not measured by their wisdom and knowledge, or Power through the Holy Spirit, it is only measured by financial and material assets.

Just because an individual is wealthy does not mean that his wealth was obtained because he has favor with God or a relationship with God. And just because an individual lives in poverty does not mean they have no relationship with God or are void of God's favor. The Bible tells us that we will know who is of Godly nature by the fruits that they bare. A person can be wealthy and be selfish, cruel, and without Christ in their lives. A person can be poor and have a heart towards God and be very giving and caring as an individual.

For the sake of this book, I am talking about and talking to the "Chosen" believer so I will focus on you who has been Chosen, because it is YOU who this book is written for.

When it comes to increasing our finances and increasing our material gain as an element of Biblical wealth, we must understand the responsibility that comes with that increase and gain. You are going to a place in your life you have never been to before. You will be on unchartered territory on this journey. Although it sounds fun and exciting, it will come with many challenges.

God wants us to be wealthy. The reason He wants us to be wealthy is not just because He loves and favors us so much. The number one reason is because He wants us to **give and share the wealth** where it is needed and secondly because He rewards us for the difficult situations that we must face on this Christian journey.

God freely gives, but He gives according to what we can handle and manage. This is the reason why not all believers of Christ are financially wealthy. Not every Christian can sit in an extremely wealthy position and not become prideful, faithless, boastful, greedy, and selfish. Not all Christians have the mental capacity it takes to handle and manage *Biblically* a large financial lifestyle. Which **requires** giving, managing, and distributing your wealth according to the will of God for your life. There are so many illustrations of this in the Bible that I have chosen not to mention any of them on this subject. Instead, I encourage you to read and study this in the Word of God on your own so you may grow in this area and can receive what the Holy Spirit needs to convey to you according to your needs and level of understanding. It is very important that you do this. How can one expect to grow and prosper in Christ but refuse to read and study His Word?

So many people want to be rich and try "get rich fast" schemes that fail and never succeed. This is because they lack the understanding of what it truly entails to be wealthy. Just like our gifts and talents are different, our levels of understanding differ as well. How much financial and material wealth we can effectively handle and manage differs from person to person. And this explains why we all are believers of Christ, yet we all have different levels and degrees of wealth and wisdom.

To become a wealthy believer, take what God is teaching you in this book and apply it to your life. "Wisdom *is* the principal thing; *Therefore,* get wisdom. And in all your getting, get understanding." Proverbs 4:7.

3

CHAPTER 3

OBTAIN WEALTH HONESTLY

There once was a man that was very active in his community promoting change for the better in the lives of the people who resided in that community. He attended church services regularly and was active in the local church. He held fundraisers to feed the homeless and to finance homeless shelters. He raised money to repair a playground for the children of that community, and every year he held an event giving school supplies to the children of that community. He was a pleasant man to hold a conversation with and seemed to have a heart of gold and a calm demeanor. He married a beautiful young lady, and they opened a restaurant in that community along with a laundromat and carwash providing jobs for those in the community while doing so. Together they had four beautiful children.

One day he was arrested and sent to prison for being a drug king pin and his wife went to prison as well. His businesses, homes, bank accounts, and all his assets were seized. His children went to foster care until family members were able to get them out and adopt them. Most people in the community had no idea this good-hearted man was a drug lord. What a shock and a loss to that community.

To all others on the outside, it seemed that this man was doing everything right in God's eyes and making an honest living. This was a good man, with a good heart, and his intentions were good, but his decision to obtain wealth in a dishonest and illegal manner was his demise. He would never make it out of prison and would die there. His decision to obtain wealth in this dishonest manner affected his wife, children, family, and community in a negative and hurtful way. He would die without his loved ones by his side. Along with that the good name, good reputation, and legacy that he built for himself, and his family was tarnished.

The moral of the story is: Obtain Wealth Honestly. All the riches of this world are temporary, and you cannot exchange it for your life or your salvation. "For what will it profit a man if he gains the whole world, and loses his own soul?" Mark 9:36.

4

CHAPTER 4

GOOD HEALTH

Wealth is not just money. Wealth also includes wisdom, knowledge, good health, joy, and happiness. Yes, I said GOOD HEALTH! Good health equals wealth!

"Behold, I will bring to it health and healing, and I will heal them and reveal to them abundance of prosperity and security." Jeremiah 33:6.

We need to be in good health and when we are not in good health, we need healing so we can be. We are talking about building wealth and success, and it is not going to be very easy to do that if we are in poor health.

In case you forgot, I would just like to remind you that the Bible is our tool and guide to living a successful life here on Earth. The Bible talks a lot about the importance of our health being in good condition. Being that our health condition is important to God, it also needs to be important to us.

The Bible gives us guidelines for our physical health, spiritual health, and even our mental health. In 1 Corinthians chapter 6, Paul tells us in the Bible that our body is the temple, the dwelling place, of the Holy Spirit. Being that God has sent the Holy Spirit to live in us to help us through our journey here on

Earth, we do not belong to ourselves, but we belong to God. Like our children belong to us with our blood and DNA running through their veins, we are the same in belonging to God. We are His children.

Paul goes even further to say that we mean so much to God that we were bought at a price. In those days they used slaves for labor, and I feel Paul worded the passage this way so the people would understand the seriousness of the obligation they had to God. Like slave owners who purchased slaves for their labor, and the purchased slaves became their property, just as much as the cattle and livestock were their property, so were the slaves. Once the slaves were purchased and paid for, they were obligated to the purchaser to work and provide labor in any capacity they were told to do. They must serve their master.

It really is not Biblical that we do with our bodies what we want to do. When we do so we are giving into those fleshly desires that do not honor God. Once we become a Christian, we are filled with the Holy Spirit that lives in us. We are to obey the Word of God at that point, not giving in to our own desires and not yielding to the temptations of this world. By doing this we are glorifying God, to whom we belong, with our body and spirit.

The price that was paid for us was done with the act of Jesus dying on the cross to free us from our sins. In exchange for this act, as a Christian, we are obligated to God's will and service. An Earthly and somewhat modern-day way for me to illustrate an example of this scenario for the natural mind to understand would be as follows: Let's say you got into a situation that caused your life to be at stake. You are about to be killed for something you did or didn't do and someone else decides to take the bullet for you and spares your life because you have a family and a career that is important in our society. In return you are indebted to that person's parents to take care of them and provide what they may need because their child gave their life to save yours. That was the exchange, because their child gave their life so you may live, you are obligated to care for his or her parents as if they were your own.

We are to honor God with making good healthy choices for our body for three reasons. We owe it to God to do so because his son sacrificed His life for us, and also, we are the temple in which the Holy Spirit dwells. And thirdly, we cannot carry out His purpose for our lives if we are not healthy mentally, spiritually, and physically.

5

CHAPTER 5

REMEMBER THE SABBATH

Some years back I was actively pulpit preaching and speaking at different churches and events. I was invited to speak at a Seventh-Day Adventist Church which was primarily a Philippine congregation at the time. The church service was held on a Saturday. I was raised Baptist but attending a non-denominational church at the time, and I was accustomed to our church services being held on Sunday mornings. Some modern-day non-denominational churches have a Saturday evening service and now I personally do love having the option to go either Saturday evening or Sunday morning.

My speaking engagement at the Seventh-Day Adventist Church went so well that the pastor asked me if I would come onboard as a pastor in his church. He offered to send me to school to get the teachings and training that they require for the pastoral staff of the Seventh-Day Adventist denomination. Although I was flattered, I declined his offer for several reasons, and one being that at that time I was accustomed to going to church on Sunday and another I was not interested in changing my denomination. He was very nice about everything, but he asked if I would promise him one thing. I asked what it was, and after he told me what it was, I gave it a few seconds of thought and then replied yes, I promise I will do that.

He asked that I promise to teach about the 4th commandment when I ministered the Word of God. Being that I agreed to do so, I had to study about it so I could have a full understanding of its importance. The 4th commandment is found in the book of Exodus 20:8-10. The New International Version says, "Remember the Sabbath day by keeping it holy. Six days you shall labor and do all your work, but the seventh day is a Sabbath of the Lord your God. On it you shall not do any work."

God is saying we need to have a balance in our life. One day a week take a day to worship the Lord freely, without time constraints or the pressures of life, take this day and just rest and enjoy worshipping and the blessings of the Lord. Do not work 7 days a week, take that Sabbath day and do no work. Sabbath means "to rest from labor; the day of rest."

How can you enjoy a healthy life if you just work, work, work, work? You cannot because eventually your body will give up and you will invite fatigue, stress, and illness into it. No one can operate at their full potential if they are not healthy. Incorporate a healthy balance in your life and rest on the Sabbath. Take that day and just worship and praise God for all He has done and is doing in your life. Praise and worship are also instrumental in maintaining our Spiritual Health. I always feel so good and refreshed after I have worshipped God with praise and song.

6

CHAPTER 6

DIET AND EXERCISE

In Proverbs 25:27 we read that "it is not good to eat much honey". Many of us have an insatiable love for sugary foods. Me included. Sugar may be addictive. There are times I have not had any chocolate in a while, (usually a short while), and I feel like I will have a mental meltdown if I do not have some chocolate! Some medical studies suggest that sugar is as addictive as cocaine. Sugar causes our body to release dopamine in the brain. Dopamine is a hormone associated with happiness and helps regulate our mood. It is released in our body during pleasurable activities such as sex, exercise, eating foods, and certain drugs are also stimulants of dopamine release. Too much Dopamine can lead to mental illnesses such as hallucinations and schizophrenia. The known long-term health effects of too much sugar include obesity and diabetes.

Diet plays a huge role in our physical health. We need to eat healthy balanced meals that includes portion control to help reduce the risk of physical health problems. Eating healthy also helps with energy levels and sleep patterns. It is good to watch your caffeine intake when considering sleep patterns and energy levels. It is not good to overly indulge in food. Doing this will also cause health problems. You should only eat what your body needs.

Exercise is necessary in maintaining good physical health. Exercising helps to tone and strengthen your muscles and builds up your energy and endurance levels. Exercise helps your cardiovascular system perform at a more efficient pace by providing oxygen to your tissues. With a healthy heart and healthy lungs, you can walk more efficiently in your Divine Purpose.

7

CHAPTER 7

MAKE GOOD FOOD CHOICES

In the book of Genesis God tells us that every seed-bearing plant on the face of the whole earth and every tree that has fruit with seed in it is ours for food. He also said in Leviticus, we must distinguish between clean and unclean living creatures that we eat. He named examples of unclean animals being pigs, rats, and anything in the seas or rivers without fins or scales and bottom feeders. We must be careful about the foods that we eat and make good decisions with our food choices for a healthy body. The Bible tells us not to overindulge in food and alcohol. Not only does it defile our bodies as the temple of the Holy Spirit, but it drains our bank account. "Do not join those who drink too much wine or gorge themselves on meat, for drunkards and gluttons become poor, and drowsiness clothes them in rags." Proverbs 23:20-21.

Here are a few more passages on the consumption of liquor and alcohol:

"Wine is a mocker, Strong drink is a brawler, and **whoever is led astray by it is not wise**." Proverbs 20:1 NKJV.

"Who has anger? Who has sorrow? Who has contentions? Who has complaints? Who has wounds without cause? Who has redness of eyes? Those who linger long at the wine. Those who go in search of mixed wine. Do not look on the wine when it is red. When it sparkles in the cup. When it swirls around smoothly. At the last it bites like a serpent, and stings like a viper. Your eyes will see strange things. And your heart will utter perverse things. Yes, you will be like one who lies down in the midst of the sea, or like one who lies at the top of the mast, saying: They have struck me, but I was not hurt. They have beaten me, but I did not feel it. When shall I awake, that I may see another drink?" Proverbs 23:29-35. Doesn't sound too wise to me.

Some people have a hard time dealing with the cards that life deals to them. Addictions can form as a way to cope with the pain of life. In comes the demon of overeating and food indulging, and for others the ugly demon of alcoholism. It is necessary to eat, and overeating becoming an addiction is often overlooked because of the necessity to give our bodies food. Drinking alcohol is also widely accepted in society and a social norm. It is customary that alcohol and food are served at almost every social function people attend. We must eat in moderation and not be prone to excessive alcohol consumption to avoid developing an addiction to either. Because this particular subject is about making good food choices, we are focusing on these two addictions.

Not only is what we eat important, but it is also important to be careful about how much we eat. Most of the diseases and health issues people suffer from are a result of overeating and poor eating habits. Alcoholism is a disease of the brain and can lead to other diseases such as liver disease. It is an illness that is chronic, progressive, and sometimes fatal. The consumption of too much alcohol impairs our judgement and opens the door to all kinds of demonic influence. Both addictions can lead to other serious illnesses and death. Both diseases are treatable and may require ongoing treatment. Both are apparent distractions in wealth building.

Drug abuse and drug addiction is also a chronic disease that has the same negative affect on our bodies and our mental awareness as alcoholism. Drug use destroys brain cells and brain cells do not reproduce. It affects and impairs functions of the brain that include learning, judgement, decision-making, memory, and behavior. No one can operate at their full potential with any kind of brain impairment. Please do not do this to yourself and get professional help if you have any type of addiction or suspect you do. Deny your pain the ability to continue to hold you hostage to any form of addiction. Break Free.

8

CHAPTER 8

SEXUAL SIN

There is an act of sin that can also affect our physical and mental health negatively. That sin is sexual sin. It is the only sin that we can commit that is done directly to our own body.

"Flee sexual immortality. Every sin that a man does is outside of the body, but he who commits sexual immorality sins against his own body. Or do you not know that your body is the temple of the Holy Spirit who is in you, whom you have from God, and you are not your own? For you were bought at a price, therefore glorify God in your body and in your spirit, which are God's." 1Corinthians 6:18-20.

Physically, we run the risk of sexually transmitted diseases when we take part in sexual sin. For some diseases there are cures and sadly for other diseases there is no known cure. There is also the risk of unwanted pregnancies.

Mentally, sexual sin opens the door to so many hurts. It can lead to sexual addictions, and it can directly alter an individual's whole personality. It can bring on anguish and confusion that people never heal from. It damages relationships and violates commitments.

Spiritually, it grieves God because we are choosing to follow our own desires instead of the leading of God's will for our lives. Then, we have how it affects *us* spiritually. Sex forms a "bond" or "union" between the male and female, a "bond" or "union" that is only intended for husband and wife. The female is the receiver who receives the male and his ejaculation, while the male is the depositor. During penetration the two are connected and become one. I believe there is a transferring of "energies" or "spirits" that takes place during sexual intercourse. It has been my experience that connecting with someone in the highest form possible, which is sexual, is not healthy spiritually outside of marriage. The transferring of their spirits, and the transferring of the type of energies that was in them, left me emotionally hurt and drained and I felt disconnected to God.

There is a term for this, and it is called: Soul Tie. A soul tie is the spiritual link that is formed between two souls during sexual intercourse. "Or do you not know and realize that when a man joins himself to a prostitute, he becomes one body with her? The two, it is written, shall become on flesh." 1Corinthians 6:16 AMP. Once you have united into one through sex, it is a soul tie. In marriage, a soul tie is lawful, and God blesses the union. In the union of the two not married, God does not bless the union, and each person is open to the transferring of demonic spirits between each other. Imagine all the people you have soul ties with and all the demonic spirits that was transferred to you. The good news is that all soul ties can be broken by the power of Jesus Christ.

It is wise to avoid inviting demonic spirits and negative energy into your temple. The stress and heartache associated with the invitation is a stumbling block to reaching our goals. It takes time to heal from that and during that time you cannot give your all to your own advancement.

9

CHAPTER 9

MENTAL WELL-BEING

"A cheerful heart does good like medicine, but a broken spirit makes one sick." Proverbs 17:22. It is always a pleasure to be greeted by someone that is cheerful, smiling, and pleasant. If we are having a bad day ourselves, just the cheerfulness of someone else will be like a dose of pick me up medicine. When we encounter someone who is down and has an unpleasant attitude it rubs off on us, and we find ourselves frowning and wondering what is wrong with that person; Who rained on their parade?

A broken spirit does make one sick. Depression is a sickness, and stress can cause illness that may lead to fatality. With all cause, it is necessary to try to avoid stress in our lives and try to live a life that is as stress free as possible. Eliminate the stress.

When you feel yourself getting down and out, read scriptures and material that will lift your spirits. Learn to minister to yourself. Learn to encourage yourself. Love yourself enough to put yourself first. You are no good to anyone else or society if you are depressed or stressed out. You cannot reach your goals that way because you won't be interested in achieving goals in that state of mind. Pray for the peace that you need in those moments and God will answer your prayers. "And the peace of God, which transcends all understanding, will guard your hearts and your minds in Christ Jesus. Finally, brothers, whatever is true, whatever is noble, whatever is right, whatever is pure, whatever is lovely, whatever is admirable—if anything is excellent or praiseworthy— think about such things." Philippians 4:7-8.

I love the way the scripture says, "the peace of God, which transcends all understanding". It is a peace beyond a normal peace. It is a peace beyond the feeling we have when everything is going our way, or the peace we have when we are in a quiet moment and can hear nothing but nature. It is a peace that is beyond that. A peace so great we cannot even understand such a peace with our human minds. Our mind is a playground for negative thoughts. Demonic influences plague our mind. But God, let me say that again, BUT GOD will guard our hearts and minds with a peace wrapped in Christ Jesus that sustains us beyond our own comprehension. I heard somebody describe their experience of this peace like this, "Thank God I don't look like what I've been through." Another said, "I could have lost my mind, a long time ago." But God.

Meditate on things that are good and pure. Don't entertain negative thoughts, guilt, past hurts, or jealousy. Don't sit in your anger. Forgive yourself and forgive others for things that get you down. Turn it around by seeking out the good in the situation and learning the lesson that needed to be learned, instead of dwelling on the negative aspect of it. You give life to what you think on. Kill the negative and give life to the positive.

This journey called life is not an easy road to travel for anyone. We all encounter some kind of heartache, bumps, and bruises as we travel through life. How you respond to those upsets and setbacks is the key to overcoming them successfully. It's hard to be up and positive all the time. The sun doesn't shine every day, it rains sometimes. But where is it written that rain is a bad thing? Storms come sometimes, but how we prepare and respond in the time of storm is the key to weathering the storm successfully.

The first key to responding appropriately is the understanding that life throws us curve balls. Life just is not going to be smooth sailing all the time.

Understand that. Everything will seem to be going well and then, boom, you are hit with something that causes you great distress or heartache. When this happens, assess the situation. Seek out what you can do to overcome the pain of it and do that immediately. Find the good in it and let that be the focus. Find the lesson in it and learn what you can learn from it. Encourage yourself while doing all of this. Tell yourself good things and think good things about yourself. And most importantly, pray your way through. Before you know it, you will be up and operating as your usual joyful self.

I am hoping you display a spirit of joy towards others. It is no need to be crabby and make life miserable for those around you. Turn your attitude around and be determined to be a joy and light in the lives of others. There is a special blessing in being that kind of person.

Never let other people's opinion of you get you down. This is hard to do, and I am very understanding of that. We want people to have a positive outlook on us and how we live our life. But the truth of the matter is someone is always trying to bring you down and tarnish your name. The hurtful truth is the person doing that is usually someone close to you or family members. Despite their efforts to bring shame to you, be confident in who you are and let only your own opinion of yourself matter to you. God says that we are fearfully and wonderfully made. Know that you are just that. Keep on improving who you are, wherever you are in your life, it doesn't matter because it's always room for improvement. We are human and we make mistakes, we make bad decisions, and poor choices sometimes. But the good thing about that is those things don't define who we are, and never let anyone else use those things to portray you in a negative light. Be truthful and admit that you have not been perfect in your life and made some bad choices, and with the knowledge you have now, you have learned from those bad choices, and you are moving onward to greater things in your life. You are not the only person who has taken the wrong path for a time, and you will not be the last. Those pointing a finger at you are not free from a life of sin and bad choices either.

Keep your mental health in check. If you need counseling and/or therapy, go and get that. Treat yourself to all that you need to maintain an optimistic and healthy outlook on your life. If you need medication to help maintain your mental health, don't be ashamed of that. More people than you think take medicine to help with their mental stabilization. If you have a situation that has you down, grab an herbal supplement to help you through. One that I use sometimes is called St. John's Wort. You can take that to help you maintain a better mood. Do what you need to do to keep a good mental balance and positive outlook on your life. Smile and be merry as you travel your road to success.

When you feel good about yourself it gives you the ability to think clearly, make healthy choices and decisions, and your ability to create wealth increases. When you have a good sense of value it increases your level of self-empowerment which drives you to create and attract wealth. Your drive and determination to achieve your goals and aspirations are at an all-time high at this point. On the contrary, when you feel low about yourself your ability to create and make money producing decisions are dimensioned immensely. Keep your self-esteem and self-worth at a high level to achieve your wealth building strategies. That's a key to success!

10

CHAPTER 10

SEEKING GOD FIRST IN ALL YOU DO

One thing we know for sure is that we will not be here on Earth forever. We are not immortal creatures. Mortality will come and we will cease to exist on this planet. As a believer in Christ, our goal is to achieve Eternal Life with Christ. Although we will not live forever on Earth, the Bible explains to us that we can live forever in Heaven with Christ. Not in a physical sense but in a spiritual sense. Our spirit man will live an Eternal existence, and our body will decay and be without life ever again. The reason our goal in death is to live an eternal life with our Father in Heaven, is because the alternative is to live an eternal life burning in Hell with Satan.

Not everybody nor does every religion believe this to be their truth. Some believe in Heaven and believe Hell is here on Earth. Others may not believe in Heaven or Hell. Whatever one may believe is their right to do so, but I believe what the Bible says for the believer of Jesus Christ.

As believers of Jesus Christ, we have an Earthly goal and purpose, and we have an eternal goal for our soul or spirit man. To achieve both we need God and all the guidance and leading of the Holy Spirit. Following the Word and

Leading of God, while here on Earth, should land us our goal of spending eternity in Heaven.

Through the grace of God, we have salvation, and we are saved from the fiery gates of hell. Titus 2:11-14 says, "For the grace of God has appeared to all men. Teaching us that, denying ungodliness and worldly lusts, we should live soberly, righteously, and godly in the present age, looking for the blessed hope and glorious appearing of our great God and Savior Jesus Christ, who gave Himself for us, that He might redeem us from every lawless deed and purify for Himself His own special people, zealous for good works."

Every man has the opportunity to receive the grace of God. No one is without that opportunity. Every man has the opportunity to be lead and taught by the Holy Spirit through God's grace as to how we should live our life here on Earth. Every man.

We, who are Christians, and confess our loyalty to Jesus Christ, are His special people. We belong to Him, and we have special gifts that come along with that rite. We should show excitement to do what God has called us to do. The fact that we have received Salvation should excite us. Our debt of freedom from hell was already paid for. Candidly speaking, it is to our advantage to live a life soberly, righteously, and godly. It will not only please God and land us a seat in Heaven, but it will keep us out of bondage here on Earth. It costs us no great wealth to have this type of life. Salvation is monetarily free to receive.

11

CHAPTER 11

READING THE WORD

If we believe in Jesus Christ, then we will believe the Bible. But how will you know what the Bible says unless you read it? You can learn scriptures and Bible stories from hearing preachers and teachers recite them. Some false prophets also twist the meaning of scriptures to fit their agenda. They are aware that many Christians do not read and study the Bible. Therefore, they easily lead these people astray. But when you know for yourself what the Bible says and what it speaks to your spirit no one can misled you. The Bible tells us to study it to show ourselves approved unto God, a workman that needs not to be ashamed, rightly dividing the word of truth.

One of the things that really irritates me is to go into a store and ask for help or guidance with a product in that store, and the individual working there cannot help me or knows very little about the product that is in the store...that they are working in. The employer is paying the employee to work in the store and sell their products and the employee knows very little about what they are selling. What a waste of money, time, and effort. I love it when an employee knows the ins and outs of the products they are selling and the store that they are working in. You can ask them *anything* about a product they are selling, and they will have the correct answer for you. Time and money well invested by the employer. I feel the same way about Christianity. How can you say you are a Christian but do not know the Bible? Christianity is based on the principles of the Bible; how can you follow something you know little about? Just sounds like you want to be a member of a club to me.

Not only should you study and meditate on the Word of God just to know and follow what it says, but it is power in reading the Bible and it speaks to and ministers to your soul when you meditate on your reading of it. The power of Wisdom and Knowledge leaps out and gets down in your spirit and manifests itself in a mighty way in your life. You can't get that without studying for yourself. You will miraculously know how to solve issues in your life and how to implement goals and things you want to accomplish in your life. The power of the Holy Spirit will grow inside you and show up in situations you didn't know you could handle with such ease. Your faith will grow, and you will not be afraid to take leaps of faith that would have been mind boggling before. God will reveal Himself to you in ways you have never imagined and your relationship with the Father will become stronger and stronger as you study and advance in reading the Word of God. Your confidence in using the power of the Holy Spirit that lives in you will deepen and grow until it just becomes a way of life for you.

No one will be able to just tell you "Thus says the Lord", because you will already know what the Lord has said. They will only be able to *confirm* what you already know. But if you do not read the Bible for yourself, study the Bible for yourself, and meditate on what the scriptures are saying to you, you won't have any of this. Anybody can tell you whatever they want to about the Bible and you would not know if it said that or not. I have seen people who have no relationship with the Lord give scriptures in a condescending way, to fit whatever the point is that they want to make at the time, and in my opinion that's a pathetic thing to do. I know that sounds harsh, but it is how I feel. The Bible is not a tool for anyone to use to lash out at someone else, and it should not be used in such a way. When someone gives you a scripture to apply to your life or current situation, it should always be in a loving way and from a place of genuine help and nurture.

The most important thing about reading and studying the Bible in its entirety, is the reason you were created, and the gift that you are to leave on this Earth through your God given talent, will be revealed to you. Many people just live their life without ever knowing their purpose for being here. They never accomplish the goal that God created them to do, and sadly never thought to seek out God's will for their lives. What a shame to never know the purpose for which you were born. The fact that you are reading this book reveals you are not that person.

12

CHAPTER 12

FELLOWSHIP

As Christians we are directed by the Bible to not forsake the assembling of the saints. There are reasons for this that are important in our walk with the Lord. So many people do not go to church or gatherings of other Christians. They are missing out on the presence of God that only shows up during the assembling of the saints. As a Christian we should want to experience our Savior in all of His fullness and availability to us. This includes how the Holy Spirit manifests Himself when two or more are gathered together in His name, meaning they have come together for the purpose of worshiping God, praising God, and learning about God.

God listens and hears our individual prayers. But there are certain times when our individual prayers alone won't work. There are times we need several saints to pray to move the mountain we are trying to move in our lives. We pray and praise God in our home and we feel so good and warm inside, no doubt. But then when we are in church and everybody is praising God, the Spirit of the Lord shows up and chains are broken in people's lives, healings take place, and miracles are performed. You can feel the Spirit so high and the power He brings as He is definitely in the building. This cannot happen individually; it requires several people to come together to witness this level of the presence of the Holy Spirit.

It's good to study the Bible with other believers. One person can bring up a passage or scripture and God will start giving revelations to all those attending. Then another person will tie in a different scripture shedding even more light on God's Word and everyone is just being fed and full of learning in a way they could not have gotten in their alone time of study. Many people feel they learn more when studying the Bible with other people than they do when they study alone. It's as though the grace of God just sheds a different and much greater understanding when there is a corporate study of His Word.

Christianity is built on the assembling together. In the Bible we see that they assembled together in the old and New Testament. This is our example that we should follow in the present day. We are faced with the evils and darkness of this world in our lives. We pray and ask God to help us during these times and we rebuke the demonic forces that rise against us. The Bible tells us in Deuteronomy that we can chase a thousand dark forces away individually, but two saints can put ten thousand to flight! This lets us know right there that we are not to walk this Christian Walk alone. We must join with other Christians. There is power in numbers. When we do the math, we would say one person puts one thousand to flight, then two people will put two thousand to flight, right? That's not the way it is counted in the Bible, two people can put eight thousand more to flight! If two people can put ten thousand demonic forces to flight from our lives, imagine the miracles that take place when you are in a church full of folk during a corporate prayer! Do what you need to do in your alone time with prayer and studying, but don't forsake going to church on a regular basis because you can experience the power of God in a way you can't when you are alone. You are doing yourself a disservice when you don't go to church, you are cheating yourself from the full power of the Holy Spirit in your life.

God has two different kinds of presence that He gives us. One is with the individual and the other is with a group of two or more. The way God meets us in our private room is not the same way He shows up in the sanctuary. In

Mathew 18:20 the Lord says, "For where two or three are gathered together in my name, there I am in the midst of them." When several people are together, and someone begins to pray, the prayer is geared towards God's will for the congregation and not towards their own personal desires. Have you taken notice to the difference from when you pray in church from when you pray in an assembly of Christians? God's will for our lives is what is the most important prayer we should pray especially corporately; we are not to be selfish and focus on our own selfish desires. When two or more people are together the power of God operates differently. The more you assemble together, the more you learn. The more you meet together the stronger your walk and faith will become with the Lord. If a new Christian does not attend church or the assembling of other Christians, he will more than likely back slide and go back to his worldly lifestyle. It is crucial that a babe in Christ goes to church to maintain his new life as a Christian, and its crucial seasoned saints be there to help teach and carry the new Christians as well as each other.

I have found that a good Bible based church will give you the courage and strength that you need to walk towards your destiny. The Word that is preached will sustain you for that week as you face the woes of life. The praise and worship will give you the confidence to continue to press towards your goals. It's motivational. People pay motivational speakers a lot of money just to hear the speaker give them encouragement. If you are in a good word church, you can get this for free! You only need to give your tithes and offerings when the basket is passed around. A much smaller price to pay for so much more received.

There is accountability in the church. Well, it should be. You can share your struggles and concerns and corporately pray for one another. The elders can give corrections and guidance to those who need it. Advice and guidance that people pay for, you can have at your fingertips just by being a part of the church. Be sure to be dependable and reliable to the assembly because you are needed as a part of the body. When you notice someone is not there, call and check on them.

Once I was attending a very small congregation and I personally knew the pastor. I thought I would help out at the church by forming a drama ministry for them which included writing and directing skits and plays. The pastor was excited about me being there, so it seemed. I ended up getting sick with something like an upper respiratory infection and I could not make it to church for at least three Sundays. No one called and checked on me at all. I had a personal relationship with the pastor that had lasted for more than 10 years at that point, and he did not once check on me or have his wife or someone else make sure I was okay. I never went back. Make sure you are amongst a group of believers in the church that will hold you accountable and will reach out to you in your absence.

Back in the mid 1980's I attended a church in St. Louis, Missouri. I joined the church for the time I was in the area. Before I joined, the people in the church including the bishop were so loving towards me. They checked on me often and wanted to make sure I was doing well. I had no family in the area, and this made me feel very welcome and less alone. I decided I wanted to join the church, and they assigned me to a Deacon immediately. I was so happy to have my very own Deacon! My personal Deacon would call me often and even came to see me and would have dinner with me. The fellowship and accountability were remarkable. The advice and guidance I received from my Deacon and the Bishop was priceless and stays with me even today. It is rare to find a church with that level of accountability, especially in today's time of mega churches. I remember the system of support, guidance, teaching, and love under the leadership of the bishop as remarkable. I would be excited to go to church every Sunday. The way I felt as a young lady going to that church is the same feeling I wish for every believer to feel about the church they fellowship with, in particular new Christians. I haven't visited this church since the 80's but I'm praying they are operating with the same care for God's children as I experienced there.

We give each other strength; we encourage one another when we come together. We need that always. It is not good to try to walk this walk of life alone. God did not intend for us to live that way. When you are in church, or amongst a group of other believers, put all your differences behind you and just be there to experience the presence of the Lord collectively.

13

CHAPTER 13

NOT BEING LUKEWARM OR STRADDLING THE FENCE

In Revelation 3:16, Jesus says because you are lukewarm, neither cold nor hot, I will spew you out of my mouth! He is talking to the Christians that go to church and believe the message but are not sold out for Christ. These Christians just live day to day without the thought of living for Christ, instead, they live for themselves. They are not concerned with operating in God's purpose and will for their lives, they just go to church, and they may just go to church *sometimes.*

These types of Christians are straddling the fence as it seems they have one foot in the church and the other foot in the world. They go to church for social reasons when they do go. There is no evident relationship with God, no prayer life except maybe in times of difficulty. They have no conviction about the sinful life they live.

This is not to be confused with a babe in Christ who needs time to grow and mature in their new faith, or someone who has backslidden in their walk with Christ. As Christians we do fall, and that is why we are Christians, because we are not perfect, we do sin, we do make mistakes, and we need the Lord in our lives to help us. The important thing for a fallen Christian, is to get back up, do not stay there. Every time you fall, get back up and God will restore you back to your place in Him.

After my first divorce, I fell. The pain and hurt associated with the divorce were so traumatic for me that I gave up doing ministry. Hurt took me to a place that I thought I would never go. I abandoned my relationships with my close friends and family, including my mom. I would not talk to God, would not read my Word, would not meditate on scriptures, and stopped going to church. I lived my life as though I had never known Christ. But there were people who knew that I was a minister and knew that I was zealous for God and now they saw me living differently. I made wrong choices during this time, and I did not care because of the fallen state of mind I was in. I was not lukewarm or straddling the fence, I had fallen into a backslidden state. God patiently waited for me to get back up. He protected me, provided for me, shielded me from the enemy even in this fallen state where I was entertaining fleshy and worldly desires and totally ignoring Him. He was there still...waiting.

On our quest to live a successful life we will notice that we will become passionate about the things we believe in and the goals we are working towards. As a Christian we are believing God to pave the way for us to accomplish this as we go forward. That requires us to develop and nurture our relationship with the Lord. Along with reading and studying the Word of God, we must avoid sin. Avoid even being in places where non-believers congregate and participate in sinful acts.

My dad told me that if I was going to do something, I needed to be the best at whatever it was I was doing. He would say, "If you are going to be a bum, be the best bum! Don't halfway do anything!" He was speaking to me halfway doing my chores at the time, but this stuck with me through life. I am passionate about my ministry and the things God has called me to do. I always give my all and if I think I will not have that fire or passion for something, I don't do it. All or nothing. This is what Jesus is saying, give Him your all or nothing. It's dangerous to be a "Sunday Saint" or lukewarm, it's dangerous to straddle the fence when it comes to your Christian lifestyle. I believe it confuses the non-believers. They say things like, "the people in the church are worse than the people in the world, so I'll just stay away from the church and that Jesus stuff'. Because lukewarm Christians are professing Christianity, but their daily lifestyle and the company they keep is that of non-believers. Most of them do not even realize this is the case for them. They think everything is okay and that they are in a right standing with God, and God is going to spew them out.

I encourage you to not become stale in your walk with God. Always be zealous for the Lord while continuously pursuing His will for your life. Notice His artwork on our planet, the wonders of nature. He is the Master Artist! Talk with Him and listen when He speaks to you in various ways. You are special to Him so show your gratitude towards Him. Continue to draw nearer and nearer to Him. Watch how He blesses you. This is so pleasing to God.

14

CHAPTER 14

MONEY

Do not allow money or getting money to be your motivation. While striving to become a wealthy believer, money is not the motivation. We belong to the Kingdom of the Most High God. He is our Ruler and King. Our God is rich and owns EVERYTHING under the sun. We are already rich because our Father in Heaven is rich. We are Aires to the Kingdom. The riches of the Kingdom belong to us, we must know, and implement the keys to access it, obtain it, and maintain it. (Which is the purpose of this book). Building Kingdom wealth is not just money. It is wisdom, knowledge, good health, joy, and happiness. Obtaining money is just one of the elements of wealth building.

Money is not the root of all evil. This is not what the Bible says. The Bible says, THE LOVE of money is the root of all evil. "For the love of money is a root of *all kinds of evil*, for which some have strayed from the faith in their greediness and pierced themselves through with many sorrows." 1 Timothy 6:10.

15

CHAPTER 15

THE LOVE OF MONEY

After Hurricane Katrina hit New Orleans a lot of the citizens of New Orleans permanently moved to other states and cities. One proclaimed Christian man who was a Katrina victim, decided not to return to New Orleans or Louisiana at all. He wanted to remain in Houston, Texas, and start his own business. When asked why he chose Houston, he said he saw nothing but money in Houston and he wanted to get all the money he could. He said New Orleans did not give him that same opportunity. Over the course of time, he talked less about God and seemed consumed with the different businesses he was trying to start to get money. In the process, his family fell apart, and he lost his wife to divorce. He never really became successful in getting a lot of money. Every endeavor he tried would work for a while and then plummet. Then he just disappeared, and no one knew where he went.

He never mentioned anything about his quest for money being God's will for his life or even praying for God's direction as to what kind of business he should start. He confessed to being a Christian but there was no God in his quest to become rich suddenly. He clearly was being greedy, and this mindset brought him sorrow and disappointment.

People rob banks, stores, and even other people because of their greed for money. People shoot and kill other people because money was the root. Great business partnerships bankrupt over disagreements of the division of money. Marriages end in divorce over money, the lack of, as well as the love of...money.

"Let your character or moral disposition be free from love of money {including greed, avarice, lust, and craving for earthly possessions} and be satisfied with your present {circumstances and with what you have}; for He {God} Himself has said, I will not in any way fail you nor give you up nor leave you without support. {I will} not, {I will} not, {I will} not in any degree leave you helpless nor forsake nor let {you} down (relax My hold on you)! {Assuredly not!} Hebrews 13:5.

Do you fully trust in God? Because where there is a fullness of trust in God, there is no lack. Where there is no lack there is no need for greed only satisfaction in God's provision. Have faith and know that a workman is worthy of his hire. Meaning, once you put in the time and effort to work, you will be paid monetarily.

We need money to live in this world. Money can allow us to enjoy certain pleasures in life. As Christians, we need not devise greedy schemes to get money. We can us our gifts, talents, and efforts to work and then watch God provide. This book is not a way to show you how to create a get rich plan. This book is my guide to share with you ways to become a wealthy believer, (in every sense, not just monetarily), and how to maintain a successful life. Money is not the motivating element in this book. Living a true lifestyle as a chosen believer and follower of Jesus Christ, and how to tap into all that comes with that, is the motivation for this book. Living our full potential as a Christian by using the gifts and talents that God has given us to carry out His will and purpose for our lives. This is the motivation for this book.

"Command those who are rich in this present world not to be arrogant nor to put their hope in wealth, which is so uncertain, but to put their hope in God, who richly provides us with everything for our enjoyment. Command them to do good, to be rich in good deeds, and to be generous and willing to share. In this way, they will lay up treasure for themselves as a firm foundation for the coming age, so that they may take hold of the life that is truly life." 1 Timothy 6:17-19.

We do have people who are rich with monetary gain in this world. Believers and non-believers alike. It's nothing wrong with being rich or obtaining riches. As wealthy believers we are told not to be arrogant, and we are to be generous givers and do good deeds for others. When we do this with a cheerful and willing heart, we are securing our place in Heaven. Here on earth is a temporary home and when we die, we cannot take anything here with us. Burying valuables and money in the grave with a corpse is a selfish act, the dead cannot do anything with it and the living could have been blessed with it.

The riches we create on earth are not guaranteed. We can lose everything that we have and end up in poverty at a moment's notice. Men and women have committed suicide because they went from riches to rags and could not handle the pressure of a lesser lifestyle than what they had become accustomed to. But as believers, we have our hope in God, and we are assured He will never leave us and will continually provide everything that we need.

I repeat, **do not allow money or getting money to be your motivation.** And now I am about to explain why. As a young child, I had to spend a lot of time in my bedroom. During that time, I read the Bible repeatedly. The Holy Spirit would speak to me through the scriptures and reveal so much to me, that now as an adult, I realize a mind that young should not even have had such profound understanding and interpretation of the Word of God. I was walking with the Lord and enjoying the wisdom and knowledge He was pouring into me through the scriptures, and I thought it was normal. My family did not understand when I would speak of scriptural things and my parents took me to see a psychiatrist, and for whatever reason that did not last long.

One day I was reading the book of John and God told me that He chose me. I did not choose Him, He chose me, and He created me to help others through the gift of writing that He gave to me. He showed me many people reading my books and actors bringing my writings to life on the movie screen. He told me if I decided to take the opportunity to become a Hip-Hop artist, that would be offered to me, I would gain wealth but lose my soul. And then, after some time the riches I had gained from my rap career would all fade away. He showed me water running through my fingers as an illustration. I would be left with addictions and bitterness from the harshness of the Hip Hop lifestyle I was going to experience. But then He said if I chose to live my life for Him, the riches He blessed me with and my writings, *will remain* and I will live a life free from addictions and have joy instead of bitterness.

A few years later, I wrote raps and was on the local radio station and was an opening act on stage for a few locally known artists at the time. One night I had a Satanic visit. Satan showed me all the houses and riches and fame he would give me if I did my music mainstream. I remembered what the Lord had showed me, and I began to call on His name to come and run Satan away. Satan did not look like any of the pictures we see...the manifestation he used to come to me was a very handsome young man. But it was Satan, and I knew it. He began to roar like an animal when I called on the name of Jesus, changing his handsome appearance to something more beastly and then he vanished. Suddenly, I felt such a peace and I was wondering if some angels were there in my room with me. I remember every vivid detail of all of this that took place. (I do believe telling my mom this is what landed me in the psychiatrist office!)

In my late teens, I was offered a small recording contract that would lead to a huge recording contract later. I turned it down. Immediately, I remembered what God told me and I wanted to live my life for Christ. Even as a young child I was a strong believer in Jesus Christ and His Word was already imprinted in my heart when I reached my teenage years. No way was I going to lose my soul to Satan. Even at that age, no amount of riches could influence me to live a life void of Jesus Christ.

"You did not choose Me, but I chose you and appointed you that you should go and bear fruit, and that your fruit should remain, that whatever you ask the Father in My name He may give you." John 15:16 NKJV.

Do not allow money or getting money to be your motivation. Let your doing that which you were created to do, the will of God for your life, your Divine destiny, be your motivation. Be motivated to use the gifts and talents God has given you. Trust God, the rest will come.

16

CHAPTER 16

WHAT IS YOUR DIVINE PURPOSE?

"For we are God's [own] handiwork (His workmanship), recreated in Christ Jesus, [born anew] that we may do those good works which God predestined (planned beforehand) for us [taking paths which He prepared ahead of time], that we should walk in them [living the good life which He prearranged and made ready for us to live]. Ephesians 2:10.

It is our human nature to do our own will. It is common that most people go through life making choices based on their own desires. Obeying the laws of the land, no doubt, but living a normal life as a good citizen, making decisions that best fit their choice of lifestyle. This is what is pleasing to mankind: simply doing what makes one happy.

The nonbeliever looks at the Christian lifestyle and tends to believe it is boring and takes all the fun out of that person's life. The nonbeliever feels the Christian cannot do the things that pleases him and enjoy the true activities that will put a smile on his face, instead he must follow the unappealing rules and regulations of God set forth in the Bible. If he does not, he will be ridiculed by the stuffy leaders and elders in the church. The nonbeliever chooses to pass on becoming a Christian because it will strip him of living his life the way he so chooses to live it.

Well, Mr. or Ms. Nonbeliever, your thoughts about us Christians sacrificing our happiness to walk a boring path, is so wrong. If anyone feels the children of God do not have a life because they believe in doing what the Bible tells them to do as a Christian, they are wrong in their thinking. In fact, I will go so far as to say, believers have much more of a life, on a much broader spectrum, than nonbelievers. When a Christian is walking in their Divine purpose, one cannot get any fuller in life than that. Not only is it fun, but it is highly rewarding in ways that are beyond a nonbeliever's comprehension. You must try God, to know.

My fellow Christian, I say to you, it is a must that as a Christian you make a fundamental change and walk according to the will of God. Making decisions and choices to please our own desires as a believer will not be the path that takes us to greatness. Doing as we so choose and negating to seek God's will and purpose for our lives will not make us happy, we will be very unhappy with the events that will show up in our lives because of doing so. The longer you walk on your own path, the more you will suffer. Here is the kicker: The more we walk in God's purpose for our lives, and the more we obey His will for our lives, the happier we will become inside out. Others will look at you and see the glow on your face. This walk produces peace and joy and comes with real happiness and wealth.

17

CHAPTER 17

ACCEPT AND SUBMIT

The first step is acceptance. We must learn to accept the way God has commanded His children to live. We must allow the Christian lifestyle to govern how we live our life. Secondly, we must submit ourselves humbly to the good service and perfect will of God for our lives.

Life has a way of bringing circumstances and troubles so harsh that we have no choice but to call on the name of the Lord. But once we accept that we were created with a purpose and submit to walking in that purpose by doing God's will for our life, the unnecessary heartache of disobedience will be in our past.

18

CHAPTER 18

EPHESIANS 2:10

When you cook a meal or a dish, maybe even a cake or pie, it has a purpose. The purpose is for the consumption of someone to eat it. The purpose is to give us the edible fuel we need to live. When you go to the restaurant and sit down, order off the menu your choice of food for the moment, it is with a purpose. The purpose is to eat the meal you ordered for the nourishment of your body. God created us knowing exactly what His purpose for our lives would be. Once we accepted Jesus Christ as our Lord and Savior, we would begin the process of being born again or recreated. The person we used to be died, and we became a new creature in Christ.

Our mission is to find out what God created us to do, so we may live out His Divine purpose for our lives. He already prepared the paths which we should take, ahead of time. Not only did he prepare the paths for our Divine purpose to be carried out, but He prearranged a good life for us and made it ready for us to live! This is how we have complete joy and happiness as we walk towards, and live in, our Divine purpose. This is living life to the fullness!

Do not worry that you cannot carry out this mission for your life. Do not be afraid that it is too much for you to do. You can do it! Hebrew 13:21 tells us that God will strengthen [complete, perfect] *and* make you what you ought to be *and* equip you with everything good that you may carry out His will, [while He, Himself} works in you and accomplishes that which is pleasing in His sight. This excites my soul!

We are not alone on this journey, God Himself is working in us and through us to do His will. Not only that, but He will give us the strength we need, and perfect us, and equip us with everything, not some things, but EVERYTHING good! He is going to make us what "we ought to be", we are no longer what "we used to be"!! Praise God, many of us do not want to be what we used to be. We are moving forward, growing, learning, and changing for the better. We are walking in our purpose and becoming wealthy believers! We will accomplish what we have set forth to do! Isn't that exciting to know!

19

CHAPTER 19

TALENTS AND SPIRITUAL GIFTS

To become a wealthy believer, in addition to applying the other keys to a successful life that I am showing you in this book, you must mainly use your talents and gifts. Talents and Spiritual Gifts are two different components that each of us were given.

Our talent can be something we were born with or something we cultivate and develop. We can use our talents for our own purposes or for spiritual purposes. With that enlightenment, we know that nonbelievers use their talents for their own personal purposes. Therefore, talents are given to the believer and nonbeliever alike.

Spiritual gifts are given to the believer through the power of the Holy Spirit. A nonbeliever cannot have Spiritual Gifts because he is absent from the dwelling of the Holy Spirit. These gifts are given only to be used for the edification of the Body of Christ, or to use to minister to others.

An individual can have a talent that they use for worldly motives to make a profit and then become a believer and use that same talent to profit through ministry. When that individual was using their talent for worldly purposes, they were using it without spiritual gifts. Once they become a believer, they receive Spiritual Gifts to accompany the talent they already have.

For example, Sam, a 35-year-old nonbeliever, plays the piano keyboard for a traveling rock band. One day Sam meets someone who invites him to church, and he is led by the Holy Spirit to give his life to Christ. He still plays for the rock band and travels with them but begins to feel out of place as he grows in his faith. Two years later he is offered a paid position to play the piano keyboard at a prominent church and he leaves the traveling rock band to take that position. While he is at the church, he participates in classes to help him grow and understand ministry. He begins to become interested in becoming a counselor in the daytime at the church for those in need of counseling. He takes the necessary courses and gets the necessary certifications and is given this position at the church. Now in addition to using his talent of playing the piano keyboard for the church he is also using his spiritual gift to serve in the ministry of counseling. His piano playing also becomes filled with an anointing from the Holy Spirit.

20

CHAPTER 20

SAM AND PAUL

At first, Sam was a nonbeliever as he traveled with the rock band. The rock band members, including Sam, enjoyed drugging, getting drunk, sexual immorality, and any sin they felt like participating in. In addition to this, they were full of tattoos and piercings. This is Sam's past history. Sam still has his tattoos, some piercings, and his memories. Although Sam no longer partakes in the sins of his past, his past has become his testimony. Sam is now able to reach other nonbelievers who are of the same lifestyle he used to live and bring them to Christ with his testimony. He can reach this genre of people because he was just like them once. Sam wrote a book about his journey and transformation that became a #1 best seller. Sam has been blessed by God to become more successful and obtain more wealth than he ever imagined.

Sam's life is also an example of why it is not good to criticize and frown upon nonbelievers and believers for what you see on the outside. The nonbeliever can one day become a believer, and all believers have a past, it is not wise to condemn, ridicule, or judge people because of their outer appearance. This is what foolish people do.

A chosen believer can also use their talent and spiritual gifts to build wealth in a non-ministry capacity. Let's look at a young football player we will call Paul. Paul grew up in church and had many spiritual gifts including a very strong faith in God and he sang in the choir. He was also a star player for his high school football team. Paul received a full scholarship to play football for a division 1 university. His senior year of college he was drafted into the NFL. Paul played many years in the NFL and continued to excel in his spiritual growth. He led many of his team members to Christ and became a chaplain for his team once he retired.

Most believers use their talents in secular careers and businesses. They use their spiritual gifts in their church and in their jobs. Sam and Paul were living in their *God given purpose* for their lives. Sam was created by God with the talent of proficiently playing the piano keyboard by ear. As a nonbeliever, Sam was using his talent to play the piano keyboard to build wealth. Most of his money was spent on drugs, alcohol, women, and partying. Once he gave his life to Christ, he began walking in his Divine destiny of that which he was created to do using his talent and spiritual gifts. Building wealth as he went forward.

Paul became a believer as a young child. He began using both his talents and spiritual gifts from the age of a young boy. He started singing in the music ministry of his church beginning at a young age. He also cultivated, trained, and developed his talent for football to make it to the NFL. Paul knew from a young boy that this was the path God had set for him to take and with extraordinary faith he pursued it diligently. His monetary reward was great, and he was held with very high regards in the NFL.

1 Corinthians 12:4-11 says this about spiritual gifts: There are diversities of gifts, but the same Spirit. There are differences of ministries, but the same Lord. And there are diversities of activities, but it is the same God who works all in all. But the manifestation of the Spirit is given to each one for the profit of all: for to one is given the word of wisdom through the Spirit, to another the word of knowledge through the same Spirit, to another faith by the same Spirit, to another gifts of healings by the same Spirit, to another the working of miracles, to another prophecy, to another discerning of spirits, to

another different kinds of tongues, to another the interpretation of tongues. But one and the same Spirit works all these things, distributing to each one individually as He wills."

This passage says that every believer has different gifts and different ministries, and they all come from and through the Holy Spirit. The Amplified Bible says it this way: There are distinctive varieties of spiritual gifts, special abilities given by the grace and extraordinary power of the Holy Spirit working in believers, but it is the same Spirit who grants them and empowers believers.

Let's note that if the Holy Spirit is working with extraordinary power *in* the believer, then the believer can outwardly do extraordinary things. The same Holy Spirit that empowers one believer to operate in their gifts, empowers all believers. My grandmother would tell me, "It is no secret to what God can do, what He does for others, He'll do the same for you."

This biblical passage goes on to list some of the gifts that believers are given through the Holy Spirit. It tells us that the Holy Spirit distributes these gifts to whoever He wants, it is not something that we can choose or learn, and each believer is given various amounts of gifts individually by the Holy Spirit's choosing. A believer can have wisdom, knowledge, and must have some level of faith. But when a believer is given the *gift* of wisdom, the *gift* of knowledge, and/or the *gift* of faith through the Holy Spirit, it is on a magnified level beyond anything ordinary.

The Bible list these few gifts of the Spirit that we read in 1 Corinthians 12. Keep in mind these are gifts of the Holy Spirit and although they can be done within our natural state, a person is not operating in the *gift* of the Holy Spirit unless it is done *through* the Holy Spirit with a Supernatural power. There are also these gifts of the Spirit: Apostleship, Evangelism, Giving, Hospitality, Pastoring, Serving, Joy, Teaching, Helpers, Leadership, Encouraging, Mercifulness, and Administration. In Ephesians 1:17 the Bible says there is the gift of the Spirit of Revelation. The gift of Mutual Encouragement is found in Romans 1:11-12. The gifts of Serving, Teaching, Encouraging, Contributing, Leadership, and Showing Mercy, are found in Romans 12:7-8. The gift of Witnessing Power is found in Acts 1:8. Earlier in this book I explained to you about Joy only coming through the Holy Spirit, and that makes it a gift from God, and it is Supernatural. You can find this in 1 Thessalonians 1:6.

In 1 Corinthians 7:7-9, Paul tells us there is a gift of Marriage and a gift of Celibacy. I interpret this to mean Celibacy while single for this believer is a gift from God, whether the person wants to be single or not, God grants them the Supernatural power through the Holy Spirit to be celibate for the purpose of ministry and the edification of the church. The gifting of Marriage in Christ, (as two believers joined in matrimony), is also a gift from God and this too is necessary for the purpose of their ministry and the edification of the body of Christ. There is an ordinary/normal marriage, and then there is the Supernatural gifting of marriage. This married couple has a special bond, a strong love, and a special connection above that which would be perceived as a normal married couple.

God declares in Exodus: "And I have filled him with the Spirit of God, with wisdom, with understanding, with knowledge and with all kinds of skills—to make artistic designs for work in gold, silver and bronze, to cut and set stones, to work in wood, and to engage in all kinds of crafts." Exodus 31:3-5 NIV. Believers who have trades and skills are no less important than others that have ministry and theological positions. All of it is from God and He honors their creativity, and so should we. Do not disregard someone's craftmanship as beneath someone in a leadership or a highly publicized position.

Have you ever been on a cruise ship? I am always so amazed at the staff that work on these cruise ships. There are thousands of people on the ship day in and day out. Yet the wait staff will remember my name and what I like to drink with my dinner after only telling them one time. Every day I am greeted by my name, and I have a hard time remembering their name. I must peek at their name tag to get their name right! The cruise ship staff work so hard to entertain the guest and to make the guests cruise experience as magically fun as possible. Always pleasant, smiling, and accommodating. Each division of the cruise ship staff has *mastered* their craft and skill in the position they are working in. Mastered *beyond* what we, who do not work on cruise ships, would ever give to any employer. With much less pay from the Cruise Line, I might add. And what disappoints me, is how often I see the guest talk down to the cruise ship staff and treat them with little to no respect, having no appreciation for the craftsmanship of the cruise ship worker. That is not an honorable thing to do to anyone.

God's children are blessed at any level of income just for walking in their purpose. Some believers are Nurses, Probation Officers, Delivery Drivers, Mechanics, Stockers of a store, Door Dashers, Lawn Care workers, Lyft drivers, it does not matter what your talent or skills are, God will bless you financially just for walking in your calling. You will find peace, joy, and comfort at any level of income. The rich should not look down upon someone with less material wealth. Circumstances and financial status do change for the rich and the poor alike.

If you are not sure of what your Spiritual gifts and individual talents are, pray and ask God to reveal them to you. What you dream about, what you have visions about, and passions about things that you find you have, all may point to your talents and gifts. You must know what your Divine purpose is on this Earth. You will use your gifts and talents to fulfill your purpose, and your wealth will be created that way.

"Do you see a man skillful *and* experienced in his work? He will stand in honor before kings; He will not stand before obscure men." Proverbs 22:29. Finally, it is important that you develop and grow in your God given gifts and talents. Learn all that you possibly can and mature in the use of them. If you do not use your gifts and talents, then you are not walking in your God given purpose. And you need to walk in the Divine purpose of your creation to achieve lasting wealth and success.

21

CHAPTER 21

SEASONS

"To everything *there is* a season, A time for every purpose under the heaven."
Ecclesiastes 3:1.

One thing man cannot control is time. Time belongs to God, and He directs and appoints every moment. Sometimes we have a season of pain, sometimes we have a season of pleasure. Sometimes we have a season of sorrow, sometimes we have a season of happiness. And it is all out of our control.

This is where our trust and faith in God is needed with our creativity. God has an appointed time, or season, for us to use certain gifts and talents. We can try when it is not our season, but that craft will not prosper. God has an appointed time and season for our Divine purpose.

Understand that many people, including you, have more than one purpose to walk in. More than one talent and gift. More than one way to make a difference in this world. More than one way to create wealth. But only during its appointed time.

Often with famous musicians and actors, we see they have a season where they are all over social media and the actors are in every movie it seems, and the singer or rapper is in every song on the radio it seems. Before that, they were struggling actors and musicians. Working hard on their talent but seeming to not get very far. And then boom, it is their season! And the best, and most intelligent thing to do when it is your season, is to work as hard and consistently as you possibly can. Do not sleep on this moment because it will not last forever. Seasons change.

Some people walk out of one season and into another. They go from a season of modeling to a season of acting. A season as a Register Nurse into a season as a Physician's Assistant or Nurse Practitioner. They successfully maximize both seasons, and as one season is coming to an end, they have made the necessary adjustments, plans, and steps to walk into the next season. This is what we must do to continue to create wealth and success. You must be in tune with the Holy Spirit to know when your season is changing and what you must do to prepare for your next season. I've seen too many people have a huge season and when the season is up for that particular talent, because they were not in tune with the Holy Spirit, they did not plan for the next successful chapter in their life, and they took a spiral downward financially instead. Some are able to get back up and bounce back in a later season, and others do not unfortunately.

The key to success in this area is to be prepared for when your time is up in one area, and it is time to walk into a different area of creativity. For the believer, that takes your continued relationship with God, an open mind, hard work, and a willingness to succeed.

To do this successfully you must stay focused on one talent at a time. If you are doing too many things at once, it divides your time, and you cannot concentrate on the one talent that is necessary for this particular season God has appointed for you. You will miss out on maximizing your season if you make this mistake. Know what is to come next, plan for it, map it out, but concentrate on this season to maximize the wealth while you are walking in it, for however long this season will be. Do not miss a beat, stay diligent in your season. If you do this, you will be very successful at creating wealth and maintaining it from one season into the next.

22

CHAPTER 22

MY MODIFIED PARABLE

There is a famous Biblical story called the "Parable of the Talents", in Mathew 25:14-30. A parable means it is not a true story, this was just a story Jesus created to illustrate his point or teach a lesson. I am going to use that same parable revised to illustrate a point for you.

Remember, I explained to you previously that back in Biblical days they had slaves to do the work of the land? This story is about a master and/or slave owner and his slaves and/or servants. This is my modified version of the biblical story:

The master was going on vacation to visit another country. Before he left, he called three of his servants and told them to take care of his affairs and live on his property while he was gone. In exchange for living on his lavish property they could use his instruments and their musical talents to create wealth to give to him money for rent. The master then gave each servant musical instruments appropriate for their musical talent according to what he believed their ability to handle and use each one of them would be. He gave one servant five musical instruments, another he gave two musical instruments, and the third servant he gave one musical instrument. Then the master left.

The servant who got five instruments quickly invested his money and used his talents making more than five times the money he had. In the same way, the second servant who had two instruments invested his money and used his talents, more than doubling his money. But the servant who got one instrument did not use his talent or the instrument and dug a hole, placed his savings in a jar, and hid the jar with his money in that hole instead.

After a while, the master returned home. He asked the servants how they used their talents and instruments. The first servant who had five instruments told the master how he made more than five times his money when he used his talent with the instruments. He said the crowds loved his music and he was offered to play at the synagogue daily. The master told him how well he did and how pleased he was. Because the servant was so loyal and used his creativity to make more money, he would give him more land and much greater wealth. The servant lived a wealthy life for the rest of his days. The second servant, who had two instruments, told the master how he used the instruments and his talents to more than double his money. He too shared how the crowds loved his music and allowed him the opportunity to play for weddings. The master told him he did well, and he was pleased. Because the servant was so loyal and used his creativity to make more money, he would give him more land and much greater wealth. The servant lived a wealthy life for the rest of his days.

Then the servant who had been given the one instrument came to the master and said, 'Master, I knew that you were an unfair and mean man. You harvest things you did not plant. You harvest crops from where you did not plant any seed. I was afraid I would lose my money and couldn't pay you your rent, and I hid my money in the ground to keep it from getting stolen. I did not use the instrument or my talent to make more money because I didn't have the time after I finished a day's work. Here is the money I hid for the rent'. The master answered him, 'You are a self-centered and lazy servant! You say you know that I harvest crops I did not plant and that I gather plants where I did not sow any seed. You pay more attention to my affairs than you do planning for your own future. You should have put your money in the bank to multiply with interest and invest in your future and used your talent and the instrument to make more money. Then, when I came home, I would have received the money you made from the instrument for rent, and you would still have your invested money in the bank'.

So, the master told the other servants, 'Take the money from that servant who didn't use his talent or the instrument and give it to the servant who made more than five times his money. Those who have much will get more, and they will have much more than they need. But those who do not have much due to their laziness, will have everything taken away from them. Throw that useless servant outside, send him into the darkness where people will beg and grind their teeth with pain as they work in the fields. This lazy servant went from being a rich, talented house slave, to a poor homeless field slave.

Let's say in the parable the Master represents God, and the servants are His believers. God is the Master of all believers, and the believer is called to serve God with their time, talents, and treasure. This is how my version of the parable relates to believers today: We as Christians believe in the Trinity as the God Head. The Trinity is God the Father, Jesus Christ the Son, and the Holy Spirit. Each one being the same in deity but having different roles as the God Head. Jesus Christ no longer walks on Earth amongst us, and when he ascended to Heaven, God sent the Holy Spirit to dwell inside of each believer and to operate in the Power of God through the believer. The master going to another country and giving the servants instruments represents Jesus Christ leaving Earth and the Holy Spirit dwelling in the believers (servants). It is the believer's duty to use all that God has given to them to serve within the body of Christ. They accomplish this by using their God given gifts and talents through the Holy Spirit to create wealth for themselves and to give a portion in tithes and offerings. Which is what the rent for living on the master's lavish property symbolizes.

It is a key element in becoming a wealthy believer to be a giver. We must be givers in order to receive. We must use the resources God has given us to create more wealth, give to the needy, and pay our tithes. We tithe our time, talents, and treasure to give God glory and for the building up of His Kingdom. It is all about Him because we are his servants. When it is your *time* or season, use your **talents** and/or gifts to generate wealth, and give a portion of your wealth which is your **treasure**, in tithes and offerings. In return, God will continue to bless you with even more.

Each servant received a different number of instruments according to what the master felt they could handle. This is how God is with us. Each believer has different gifts and different talents and the combined amount given to each believer varies. God gives to each believer according to what that believer can handle. Some believers have gifts and talents that are more complicated, and more in number than other believers because they can handle the stress and pressures that come with having such. To whom much is given, much is required, (Luke 12:48). When you see leaders and believers who have a lot of spiritual gifts and complicated talents, this comes with a heavy price tag. They have overcome obstacles that the average believer could not survive or remain sane if it were given to them. In return for their dedication to the service of their ministry, God gives them more. But as we see in the story, this is of no concern for the believers because they all are blessed and live comfortably at the financial level in which they reside. The two first servants had no jealousy amongst them when the master increased their blessings at different financial levels nor when one was given more instruments than the other. When these types of jealousy and envy arise amongst the saints, it does not come from one that is filled with the Holy Spirit. The saints that are Holy Spirit filled have no room for such darkness and operate only in the gift of joy for themselves and love for others.

The first two servants were not afraid to invest the money they had saved already and to go out to use their talent of playing musical instruments, to get more money to pay their rent to the master upon his return. As a result, they both landed long term permanent positions to continue to use their talent and instruments to create wealth. We must have faith and trust God when the Holy Spirit leads us to go and use our talents to create wealth. We cannot have doubt. And if you do have a little doubt or fear, muster up your courage and go anyway in faith, and watch God open the doors you need to be open because of your obedience. The power of the Holy Spirit will be working through you as it is your season to succeed. You will not fail with such Supernatural power.

Because of the obedience of the first two servants to their master, the master rewarded them greatly, for the rest of their lives. That is exactly what God will do for you when you do the very same thing.

The servant who received the one instrument did not even use the musical instrument and dug a hole in the ground and buried his money there. He did not even put the money in the bank so it could draw interest. Many believers do not use the power of the Holy Spirit that dwells inside of them. They do not operate in the power God has invested in them. That musical instrument represents an investment the master made in the servant. Musical instruments are not free. That was an investment in the servant's known talent. Surely the master knew the musical talents of the servants if he gave them instruments to play. Each one according to their talent and what they could handle. What a waste when Christians do not use or cultivate their gifts, and do not become more experienced in their talents. They just live day to day never walking in their calling or fulfilling their purpose. All that power invested in them through the Holy Spirit, and they do not touch it. I am always hearing of someone investing money in another person's talent and that person does nothing but blow someone else's investment. That is what we are doing to God when we do not use our God given talents and gifts to walk in our purpose. We are blowing His investment in us.

Then the servant had the nerve to try to tell the master his faults. Saying the master is unfair and mean, he harvests where he does not sow, he gathers where he has not planted seeds. So, out of fear for the master he buried his money and did not use the musical instrument. This man came with excuses. How mean and unfair could the master be if he invested in this man? Should that have even been the man's concern? This is why the master called this servant self-centered and lazy because he did not share his musical talent with others, he didn't even try. All he was thinking about was his own self. Sitting in the master's lavish home complacent because he was too lazy to minister with his gifts and talent. On top of that, he buried the money in the ground instead of putting it in the bank to draw interest or invest. There are believers that make excuses as to why they will not use their talents and gifts to do what God has called them to do and do not bring their tithes and offerings into the storehouse. Therefore, the treasures that were predestined for these types of believers end up being a blessing to the believers that work hard to walk in their purpose and skillfully use their gifts and talents.

The lazy believers live their lives entertaining things of the darkness and the pains that accompany this type of lifestyle. Then they become angry and jealous of the Christians being blessed and doing well for themselves, for no other reason except they see all the blessings God has given to them. If a believer refuses to use his God given abilities for the edification of building up the Kingdom of God, he is useless to the body of believers. Those that are doing what they are created to do, do not want this type of energy in their way because it brings disruption to their ministry. If you are operating in your season, working hard to use your talents and gifts for the Lord, and a self-centered, lazy Christian tries to interrupt with some foolishness, please kindly dismiss that individual from amongst you. Believers are to be outwardly displaying the fruits of the Spirit. If someone comes with some strange fruit, do not entertain that. "You will know them by their fruits. Do men gather grapes from thornbushes or figs from thistles? Even so, every good tree bears good fruit, but a bad tree bears bad fruit. A good tree cannot bear bad fruit, nor can a bad tree bear good fruit. Every tree that does not bear good fruit is cut down and thrown into fire. Therefore, by their fruits you will know them." Mathew 7:16-20.

The master came to each servant and asked them to give him an account of what they did with the money they had and the instruments he gave to them. God holds us accountable for the resources and blessings He bestows on us. We are to be good stewards of what He has given us. The day is surely coming when we will have to give an account for how we lived our lives and how we used our talents and gifts to bless others.

"For where your treasure is, there your heart will be also." Mathew 6:21. The third servant buried his treasure in the ground. It reminded me of how we bury the dead in the ground. His treasure no longer had life. The third servant did not value the opportunity to use the gift his master invested in him, and he buried his treasure and did not allow it to grow and cultivate. His heart was not to serve his master. The servant could have used that money to make even more money. God wants us to multiply what He gives us. He expects to see growth in all areas of our Christian life. We are not to be complacent and stagnant in our lives.

The other two servants used their creativity to minister to other people. They used the power invested in them to create the music that ministered to others, and in return it created wealth, and then they gave the master the money they owed him. The power that was invested in them by the master, in this story, was the instrument. In our lives it is the Holy Spirit given to us from God above. Through the Holy Spirit we are given the power to create what will minister to other people, and in return it will bring us wealth, and then we must honor God with our tithes and offerings. And by minister, I mean whatever it is that your creativity does to meet the need of those in a particular group of interest that aligns with your talent.

A key to a successful life is to continually use all your resources to increase monetarily in your daily living. Strive to become a smarter Christian through study and fellowship; Become a wealthy Christian through continued smart investments and continued giving of your time and treasure. Continue to use your talents to create; use what you have created to increase your income and use your Spiritual gifts to minster with what you have created.

A major key to wealth is how you view money. Understand that you don't work to earn the money to pay your bills. That is not the purpose of having money. Do not think, say, or believe that you work to pay bills or to survive in this world. That is the thought process of the economically poor. The primary reason you create ways to work and make money is to use that money to make more money. That is the thought process of the economically wealthy.

With that thought process as a Chosen vessel we know that our purpose for creating more wealth is for the building of the Kingdom of God. The more we have, the more we tithe and give. We are to be the lender not the borrower; the head and not the tail; a tither and not a thief.

"Will a man rob or defraud God? Yet you rob and defraud Me. But you say, in what way do we rob or defraud You? You have withheld your tithes and offerings. You are cursed with the curse, for you are robbing Me, even this whole nation. Bring all the tithes (the whole tenth of your income) into the storehouse, that there may be food in My house, and prove Me now by it, says the Lord of hosts, if I will not open the windows of heaven for you and pour you out a blessing, that there shall not be room enough to receive it. And I will rebuke the devourer for your sakes, and he shall not destroy the fruits of your ground, neither shall your vine drop its fruit before the time in the field, says the Lord of hosts. And all nations shall call you happy and blessed for you shall be a land of delight, says the Lord of hosts." Malachi 3:8-12.

23

CHAPTER 23

NO FEAR

"For God did not give us a spirit of fear; but of power, and of love, and of a sound mind." 2 Timothy 1:7 KJV.

The Amplified Bible says it this way, "For God did not give us a spirit of timidity (of cowardice, of craven and cringing and fawning fear), but [He has given us a spirit] of power and of love and of calm and well-balanced mind and discipline *and* self-control."

The Bible tells us God did not give us a spirit of timidity which is the fear of the unknown or unfamiliar and/or the fear of making decisions and changes. You should not be afraid of embarrassment when walking in your Divine purpose, and you should not let fear hold you back from using your creativity to build wealth.

This spirit of timidity is the same as the spirit of fear. You cannot accomplish your goals and dreams with the destructive spirit of fear disabling you. You will miss out on your opportunity if you allow fear to hold you back. This is a cowardly thing to do. We are not created to be cowardly and allow the spirit of fear to govern our lives. God created us to be victorious and overcomers of all challenges. He gave us a spirit of power, a spirit of love, and a spirit of wisdom which leads us to be calm, cool, and collected when faced with the unfamiliar or the unknown, or change.

Humans are born with two fears, the fear of falling and the fear of noise. For example, we need to be afraid of falling or as a child we will walk right off a cliff or fall hard down the stairs. We need to be afraid of loud noises for the same lifesaving reasons. If a child is walking and hears a vehicle coming the fear of the sound will cause them to move out of the way. These are natural human fears given to us from birth, just like we know to eat when we are hungry from birth, this response is naturally given to us.

You may have heard people say how a baby or a child is not afraid of anything? Other than the two fears the child is born with, the child is not afraid of anything because he hasn't lived long enough to adopt any fears. The child will be startled and jump at a loud sudden noise. The child will be fearful of falling or tumbling down steep stairs. But the child will not be afraid of a snake or spider because neither of them will make a loud noise.

The child doesn't know not to touch fire until the child touches the fire and gets burnt. The child has then learned from a life experience not to touch fire because he will get burnt, or someone tells him "Fire is hot, don't touch it because it will burn you and hurt." Then the child adopts the fear of being burnt if he is to touch the fire or something hot.

This is not in any relation to the "spirit of fear" that God did not give to us. God equipped us with two natural fears, the fear of falling and the fear of loud noise. All other fears are learned after birth and are adopted throughout life from experiences and from hearing someone else tell us of being afraid of something and we become afraid of it as well.

The *spirit* of fear is different from the natural fear of falling and the natural fear of noise. The spirit of fear is also different from learned or adopted fears. We pick up abnormal fears as we grow through life and life experiences. We may hear other people talk about their fears and we adopt them, or we experience something that frightens us, and we develop a fear of that thing. Some people have adopted arachnophobia or ophidiophobia. Some people are afraid of flying in airplanes or driving on a busy highway. These are abnormal fears because they are not fears that we are born with.

Like superstitions. Maybe we heard that if we break a mirror, we will have seven years of bad luck. Then you become afraid to break a mirror to avoid having seven years of bad luck. This is also a type of abnormal fear.

The "spirit" of fear is a demonic spirit, not just an abnormal fear. A demonic spirit is a spiritual force or entity that is not the Holy Spirit which means it didn't come from God, but it came from Satan with the sole intent to prevent us from accomplishing that which God created us to do.

Demonic spirits have names that describe each individual spirit, and this demonic spirit is called a spirit of fear. Demonic spirits cause the action in the person that is the name of the spirit. Meaning the action that this spirit causes in the human is to make the human afraid, scared, timid and cowardly.

For example, the spirit of alcoholism causes the person to irresponsibly drink alcohol and too often become drunk beyond their control. This is different from just having a glass of wine with dinner sometimes and not becoming intoxicated, which is not the influence of a demonic spirit. When a person is influenced by the spirit of alcohol, they become addicts and destruction soon follows. A Demonic spirit destroys the lives of the people it has influence over.

It may sound strange, but the spirit of fear is just as destructive as any other demonic spirit. The spirit of fear will cause our minds to run rapidly with fearful possibilities. There is no peace or calmness when our mind is consumed with fearful thoughts. And when we are this afraid to walk in our destiny, we do not proceed to live according to our life purpose because of the demonic influence of the spirit of fear.

Many people have allowed the spirit of fear to prevent them from using their talents to successfully accomplish their goals and create wealth. In the modified parable I previously told to you, the man with the one talent claimed to be so *afraid* of the master's way of dealing with people that he did not use his talent or instrument to create wealth and to live out his God given purpose for his life. As a result, He ended up working in the fields the rest of his life, while being paid a minimal wage, and never walking in his destiny.

Don't let this be you. Do not allow the spirit of fear to hold you back from accomplishing your life goal and creating wealth. That which you feel a tugging to do, do not be afraid to switch and/or change what you are currently doing and to walk on a different and unfamiliar path. The Holy Spirit is directing you and will provide for you through this transformation and journey. The Bible tells us in Psalm 34:4, that if we seek God, He will hear us, and he will deliver us from all our fears. He did it for David and He will do it for us.

Courage is being afraid but doing what you are afraid of anyway. Have courageous faith, knowing that God is going to open every door that you need to be opened, and the spirit of fear will flee from you as you courageously walk in your purpose. You will find that as you do this and cast aside fear, the spirit of fear will be replaced with the spirit of power, of love, and of a sound mind. You will no longer be afraid, and you will become assured and confident as you walk in your purpose.

"Submit yourselves, then, to God. (Dedicate yourself to God's will for your life and walk in your Divine purpose). Resist the devil, (don't allow demonic influences to tempt or control you), and he (the demonic spirit), will flee from you." James 4:7.

CHAPTER 24

DISCIPLINE AND SELF CONTROL

"Like a city whose walls are broken through is a person who lacks self-control."
Proverbs 25:28 NIV.

Self-control is one of the fruits of the Spirit. Not being disciplined and exercising self-control in our lives can destroy us and crush our dreams and goals.

It must be a horrible feeling to have a habit and/or addiction of some sort and not be able to kick it or manage it, instead you have no self-control over the habit or addiction, and it is controlling you.

It must be a horrible feeling to not be able to exercise restraint and the ability to walk away when you are angry and instead you immediately become aggressive and/or violent.

It must be a horrible feeling to want to stop partaking in a knowingly sinful act but can't because you have no self-control, and instead it has consumed you.

Having no self-control can land you in jail or the grave. Imagine the thoughts and feelings of family, friends, and loved ones at the funeral of someone who died because of their own lack of self-control. Even though everyone still says nice things as part of the eulogy, it's still in the thoughts and on some tongues as to how the person died and how it could have been avoided only "if" that person had exercised self-control.

What's even worse is never fulfilling your purpose in life because of your lack of discipline and no self-control. Even if you have started the journey towards your Divine Destiny but you never complete the journey because you spiraled out of control at some point. That's a mission unaccomplished, an incomplete mission, a Divine mission aborted.

Being that self-control is one of the fruits of the Spirit, we know that this is not something we can maintain or have with our own earthly nature. This is something that will require us to have a spiritual relationship with God. We will lose the battle of temptation and fall prey to Satanic forces to crush our dreams and goals if we aren't in sync with the Holy Spirit. Flesh can't fight spiritual warfare.

When a boxer is preparing for a boxing fight, he must train. He begins to train many months ahead of time for these few minutes of the fight. He must watch what he eats, exercise, practice boxing, and study techniques for hours and hours daily until the big day. His weight can't go over his division weight limit and his body must be able to withstand the punches of his opponent. He can't begin to prepare for such a fight just a few days or a week or even a month before the fight. He starts training several months before the fight and trains in between fights to stay prepared so when another fight is scheduled, he is not out of shape. This is exercising self-control.

We must follow a similar path and spend our lifetime training to pursue our destiny. We must study the Word and know its contents because it will build faith and Christian character. It will strengthen us and prepare us for adversity. It will show us how to live and how to govern our time. We will know how to decipher right from wrong in our lives. The Word of God "teaches us to say 'no' to ungodliness and worldly passions, and to live self-controlled, upright, and godly lives in this present age". 1Titus 2:12.

There are activities that are completely legal to do that will consume our time and minds and have us falsely believing it is nothing wrong with us constantly doing whatever that thing may be. Sometimes because that "thing" we are consumed with is not seen as wrong, illegal, or a sin to do, we as Christians don't even see it as an addiction. When in fact, it is.

I can tell you of two distinct occasions when this happened to me. There was a time when I would constantly drink grape flavored soda. This grape flavored soda had to be a certain brand. I had gotten so bad with my craving for it that I had to have it every day. Then one day, out of the great blue sky, I realized I was addicted to this brand of grape soda! I proposed in my heart at that moment to kick that habit and that's what I did, that day. There was another time when my children were young, that I became drawn into daytime soap operas. I would stay glued to the TV for the hours of the day that the soap opera was on. We didn't have DVR recording or a way to watch them later, back in those days, so I had to watch TV daily at the times that the shows came on. I arranged my appointments and nap time for my children during the time the soap operas would come on. I wouldn't even talk on the phone except during commercials. If I was interrupted for some reason while the show was playing and it wasn't a commercial break, I had a major attitude with whomever disturbed me at that moment. I would allow nothing to come in between me and my soap opera addiction watching time! Once again, I realized I had an addiction to these soap operas and I decided I had to break that addiction and did so, at that moment. Never again have I watched TV like that. I have kept a quiet house free from the noise of TV for many years now. I record shows of interest and barely find time to watch them and when I do, I will pause the show if need be and most times I fast forward through the commercials. Except Superbowl, I love the commercials during Superbowl!

Since those addictions I have purposed in my mind to never allow anything to control me or consume my mind and/or time like that ever again. Drinking that soda like that was completely unhealthy for me and I try to avoid carbonated drinks. My body seems to not be able to tolerate too much carbonation and I will end up with a health issue if I drink too much of it. No way can I consciously harm myself continuously by that or any addiction. (Sweet treats and chocolate call my name very often but I refuse to allow it to become an addiction. I use self-control and although I partake of it, I am not addicted to it, and I am very aware of how much I indulge in sugary sweets, so I do not develop a food addiction).

I believe I was able to break these addictions once I realized they were a problem because of my relationship with God. I do believe my Spiritual relationship keeps me from forming addictions. I believe I may have an addictive personality and can easily become addicted to something, so I am very conscious of that awareness which increases my determination to not allow anything to control me.

"And the God of all grace, who called you to his eternal glory in Christ, after you have suffered a little while, will Himself restore you and make you strong, firm, and steadfast." 1 Peter 5:10 NIV. This scripture is so very true for me to the core. Many times, I have fallen, but I didn't stay there. Not only did I get up, but God restored me back to my place and into what I should have been doing when I fell, He equipped me with the strength to stand and remain standing.

Exercising our free will and living as we choose to do is such an easy way to live. But it comes with consequences both natural and spiritual, especially when we allow something to control or consume us. It's just wise not to live this way and to choose to use restraint. And this, my friend, takes discipline and self-control to do. Consistent prayer and meditation will strengthen you to stay free from addictions of any sort. Including sex addiction. (Because somebody needed to know that).

It's a sacrifice. Just know, in the end, the feeling that we will have once we have completed that which we were created to do, will prove to be well worth the sacrifice.

25

CHAPTER 25

READ AND SELF TEACH

Some people go through life never fulfilling their purpose. Some live in poverty all their lives. Some are born into money but are very poor at living life. The sad thing about this is that these types of people are mostly satisfied living their lives this way. They are not concerned and do not care that they are not walking in their Divine purpose for their lives. They seem oblivious to the fact that they were created by God with a purpose to fulfill in this lifetime.

Avoid being one of these types of people. You know you were created with a Divine purpose. Teach yourself everything you can possibly learn about your talents and skills. Always take part in teaching activities and mentally digest those things that are to better yourself and to learn. Listen to those that have more wisdom and knowledge in your area of learning and learn from them.

"The wise will hear and increase their learning, and the person of understanding will acquire skill and attain sound counsel [so that he may be able to steer his course rightly] Proverbs 1:5.

When should you stop learning? Never. Learning is a lifelong assignment. The longer you live, the wiser you should become because you are continuously learning. Everyone does not live their lives this way. Nor does everyone have the desire to learn and grow in knowledge.

Many people don't listen to wise counsel or sound advice. The very beginning of this scripture tells us the wise will hear. It's not wise to be the one that thinks they know it all and doesn't listen to others. It is wise to listen and increase your learning. With the internet we have so many resources at our fingertips. Use them and learn, educate yourself on the things that interest you. This is how you teach yourself.

Let's break down the scripture:

"**A wise man** [one who orders his life in accordance with the Law and Word of God] **will hear** [hearken and obey; listen], **and will increase** [add; continue] **learning** [receive instruction; be persuaded]; **and a man of understanding** [prudent; discerning; perceptive] **shall attain** [accept; buy; get; acquire] **unto wise counsels** [accept guidance]:"

And how do you start? What is the starting point of obtaining and learning this plethora of knowledge? I'm glad you asked!

The {reverent} fear of the Lord {that is, worshiping Him and regarding Him as truly awesome} is the beginning and the preeminent part of knowledge {its starting point and its essence}; But arrogant fools despise {skillful and godly} wisdom and instruction and self-discipline. Proverbs 1:7.

The answer is: You start by developing and maintaining a personal relationship with your Heavenly Father. When you start here, God sees, knows, feels, acknowledges, your heart towards Him, and He wants to bless you in so many ways as a result. One of those ways is by imparting within you the wisdom and knowledge you lack and seek. The closer you draw to Him in your relationship with Him, the more He pours into your spiritual and natural being. Spiritual because it's food for your soul. You eat and digest knowledge and have understanding so much more than before, and natural because you can walk, talk, and naturally display this wisdom and knowledge openly.

Not only is this the starting point but this is its ESSENCE. When the psalmist tells us in the Bible that this starting point of fearing the Lord, worshiping the Lord, and regarding Him as the head of our lives and knowing the awesomeness of God is its essence in obtaining knowledge, it means it is beyond necessary and essential. Without having this relationship with God, obtaining this type of knowledge and wisdom at this supernatural level is impossible. Anyone can acquire worldly wisdom and worldly knowledge, but you must have this depth of a relationship with God to acquire Holy Wisdom and Holy Knowledge. Once you walk with the Lord in this way wisdom leads you to be able to accept instruction, correction, refining, and self-discipline. This is the lifestyle of a wise and successful chosen believer.

26

CHAPTER 26

PERFECT YOUR CRAFT

As you press towards your goals and aspirations, you need to also perfect your craft and skills. Alongside getting Holy Wisdom and Holy Knowledge, get formal training and education as well. When there is an opportunity to have training or to attend workshops and the like, jump on it. Find someone that is where you are trying to be and allow them to mentor you. Pray for the right mentor to show up in your life and learn all you can. If you need a degree to help you reach a broader audience or just to help perfect your craft, skill, and/or calling, then, please go accomplish that. You cannot be a physician without a medical degree, or you may end up in jail for malpractice. Just an example.

When you know better, you should do better. The more you know about your craft the more confident you will be going forward.

When we self-teach, we may lean towards learning what we enjoy learning because it's what we have chosen to learn. But when we have formal training, we are taught beyond what is pleasing, easy, and comfortable for us. You are forced to explore areas of learning you may not have otherwise sought after on your own. So please don't despise formal avenues of learning.

The world we live in likes to see titles, degrees, licenses, certificates, diplomas, and multiple trainings, tagged on to names for accreditation. I'm not saying it is necessary, I am saying if you need that, go for it. If it will help you perfect your craft as an individual trying to learn, go for it. It's a lot more out there to learn than what you can self-teach. It's worth it to learn and grow on all levels available to you.

Never feel inadequate or "less than" because of the lack of formal training while working towards your goals. Get what learning you can, and watch God propel you forward.

27

CHAPTER 27

HICCUPS AND TRAPS

As you digest what you are about to read in this section, please give much thought to those individuals in your inner and outer circle. Inwardly retain and identify these types of individuals I am about to describe to you.

There are certain people that Satan, (forces of dark, evil, demonic, or whatever you choose to call it), places in your life that are your spiritual enemy. When it comes to spiritual warfare, they have been chosen to stir up battles within your life. These individuals are strategically picked by Satan to be a hater in your life. They can be close to you and most often are blood relation, such as a sibling, a child, an aunt or uncle, a neighbor, a coworker, or even a parent. Know who these people are. Identify them as one that is not for you but against you.

It is not wise to waste time on trying to win the favor of these groups of people. They have been placed in your life by Satan for a specific reason, during a specific season, because of the favor of God on your life. These are your haters.

Regardless of the assignment given to them by Satan to try to holt your mission, God has told us that ALL things will work together for our good if we keep His purpose for us first and foremost. Any evil or plot used against you, God can and will use it for your good.

Try to learn not to allow the purpose they have in your life to become a stumbling block for you when it comes to you working towards your destiny and doing the things that Christ has called you to do. Do not allow these people to accomplish in your life that assignment that Satan has given to them.

We know that because they are close in blood relation or proximity, that the execution of their purpose in your life is very hurtful to you but allow the insight of their hater attitude and actions to take precedence over the hurt it causes. You do this by understanding their purpose and by whom they have been sent, rather than the relation to you, and by applying the weapons of warfare described for us in Ephesians 6:10-18.

28

CHAPTER 28

THE STORY OF HAVIER

We were created to worship God. So many people enjoy worshiping God in some form of music. Havier is one of those people. His musical talent is so grand! He plays several instruments, writes lyrics and the accompanying music, and plays his instrument while singing his new creation of worship with a beautiful melodic voice.

Havier's talent has earned him several awards and visibility. He also was known for leading worship for large Mega Churches and made appearances in popular movies and TV shows.

Flying high with fame, Havier became careless and lost sight of his purpose and the purity it required of him. Married with a family, he began to spend less and less time at home and more and more time away pursuing the elevation of his career as a gospel artist.

A beautiful young lady slid into his inner circle after catching his attention. They shared a special closeness that Havier felt was needed in his life at that time. By becoming wrapped up in pursuing his career rather than his calling, his sense of discernment and willpower was gone, and he ate the fruit of the beautifully disguised trap the enemy served him.

This went on for some time without anyone knowing, and then people started to see what was happening and someone warned Havier's wife of his affair. What is done in the dark will come to light.

After confronting Havier, his wife went to the pastor of the church where he was ministering music and told that pastor of the affair. When Havier was questioned by the pastor he did confess of his affair. The pastor fired Havier from his position as minister of music and Havier shamefully left the church.

The information of why Havier left the church, and his affair spread across the entire Earth through all forms of social media and TV broadcasts, shaming Havier even more. Suddenly, the beauty of Havier's music was forgotten and nonverbally banned from Christian radio waves and was no longer being sung in churches all over the world. The respect he had gained as an influential gospel artist and leader was crushed and suddenly, his status changed, and he was looked upon by others as a person of low morals and bad character.

Havier had broken his own heart. He went into seclusion.

While in seclusion, Havier's wife divorced him. He stopped seeing the young lady he was having the affair with, and she moved on to her next chapter. Havier's relationships were now broken. In his dark place of brokenness, he couldn't find the words to say to his children, to his parents, to his friends and colleagues, so he remained in solitude for several months.

Try having compassion in this situation, and just imagine how Havier must have felt during this time. People have no mercy and can be cruel and malicious. Let's be honest, Havier is not the first to fall into this trap and will not be the last. Yet his heart is broken, his relationships are broken, and he is hiding from himself, from the world, and he is not communicating with his Heavenly Father whom he cannot hide from.

His family is hurt and torn. His church is hurt and torn. All his fans are disappointed, and his ministry is null and void. He feels no one wants to hear from him again. He stops using his musical talents even in solitude he refuses to sing or touch an instrument. On top of all of that, his income from ministry with the mega church has ceased. Havier can no longer financially support his children.

Finally, one day after many months had passed, he was feeling a little bit better about himself and he remembered when he was a younger teen, and he would sing and play for the action figures he had in his bedroom. Those figures served as his audience. He went about his apartment and lined up cologne bottles, deodorant, shampoo bottles, etc. and pulled out his keyboard and started to play for them. He continued to do this for a few weeks and then he started adding lyrics as he played. After a while he grabbed pen and paper and began to write the lyrics with accompanying music and started creating songs out of this place of brokenness.

One year into writing thirteen songs in solitude, he heard a knock on his door. Over a year later someone finally came to see about Havier. When he answered the knock, it was a long-time friend that is also in the gospel music industry as an artist. Havier welcomed him into his home as if no time had ever passed. They talked on Havier's couch for over four hours.

Havier shared some of the music he had written with his friend. On one song the friend joined in, and they collaborated on that song. His friend invited him to join in at a church event the following evening and perform the song together that Havier had written. Havier accepted the invitation, shocking his own self that he had done so.

The following evening came, and Havier had a hard time emotionally showing up for the event to perform his new song with his friend. But he showed up, and the song was so moving that it touched the hearts of so many people that evening.

Out of that one event Havier received six other invitations to come and minister his music at different events. He accepted every one of those invitations. This required him to put a band together and to get a couple of backup singers and he taught them his new music. Which lead to recording his thirteen new songs on a new album/CD. This CD went platinum.

Havier began ministering the songs he had written out of his hurt and healing process all over the world and would share his testimony as he did so. He also shed light on his concern for people in the ministry that make mistakes, and the ministry leaders tosses them to the side and leaves them with no means of income to support their families or themselves. Leaving them broken with no help to heal, scandalizing their names in the process. Havier had become an advocate for this type of treatment to those in ministry and continued to bring awareness to this concern that was pressing on his heart while ministering his music.

Eventually he met a beautiful young lady that was very loving and compassionate during his healing as he ministered in song. They began to sing together and eventually married. Havier was able to purchase a beautiful home and increase his income. God restored Havier in all aspects of his life, ministry, love, happiness, and acceptance was now prevalent.

29

CHAPTER 29

THE STORY OF CYNTHIA

Cynthia also worships God and ministers in music using her dynamic voice. She seemed to rise out of nowhere and rose to fame with her voice and ministry almost overnight.

A single mother of two young children hit the jack pot with her voice and her love for worshiping God. She landed a record deal when the right person heard her singing in a grocery store! She worked hard on a CD and when it hit the airwaves Cynthia was propelled to the top of the gospel music charts and every church and church function imaginable was trying to get Cynthia to minister at their event.

Cynthia was advised to get a team of people to work for her. She had a manager, a hair stylist, a nanny, a cook, a publicist, a voice coach, a booking agent, and the list goes on. She had to continue to do singing engagements to pay all of these people. She was constantly busy creating and ministering music for the Lord.

After a while this new busy lifestyle began to take a toll on Cynthia, and she turned to alcohol to try to cope. She witnessed leaders in the church doing drugs, committing adultery, and admitting that they were stealing from the church. Even the people that she hired, that had confessed to Christianity, were doing a lot of sinful activities and was there to make the money that could be made in that industry. She found out that her team *said* they were Christians, but some were also shady and all about the money that they made from her ministry. They continued to push Cynthia to "appear" Holy and hide her drinking addiction so the money could continue to roll in. No one in her circle confronted her and told her that she needed professional help with her addiction, and that she shouldn't continue to minister in her present condition. Instead, they found ways to "sober" her up so she would show up for her scheduled appearances.

Cynthia began to resent God for putting her in this position of ministry and the spotlight. She became angry with the people around her and feeling as though they represented all Christians with their selfish and greedy ways. It wasn't too long before Cynthia didn't want to do ministry or sing gospel music anymore. She forgot that she was created to do this very thing she was doing, and she hated every detail involved with ministry and the gospel industry.

One evening Cynthia was at the bar of the Hotel she was staying in after a singing engagement in that city. Cynthia drank so much she was noticeably drunk. She started having a conversation with the lady sitting at the bar beside her and she didn't notice this woman only had a coke in her glass. Cynthia also didn't know this lady had travel 4 hours from another city just to hear Cynthia sing in person because Cynthia was her favorite gospel artist. By coincidence they were staying at the same hotel.

Cynthia assumed in her drunken state that this lady was drinking alcohol with her and was far from being a Christian. Cynthia was in a rage as she angrily told this woman how she hated singing gospel music and didn't want to sing or minister anymore. She said the people that call themselves pastors and Christians were snakes. Church was only a business that misled the people, and the people in it were being stupid and giving their bill money to the church instead of paying their bills. Cynthia admitted to being an alcoholic to the lady without even being coerced. She told her she drinks to tune the religious people out. She wakes up drinking and drinks the entire day, every day.

This lady was a therapist by trade. As she listened to Cynthia, she felt compelled to help her. She looked in her cell phone for a nearby rehab center that would take Cynthia in if she could convince Cynthia to go. She began to minister to Cynthia right there at the bar.

She never let Cynthia know who she was and why she went there. She immediately understood her purpose from God for having her there. Miraculously she was able to convince Cynthia to get the help she needed and go to rehab. It took 5 hours of talking with Cynthia and they left for the rehab without anyone knowing.

Cynthia never knew the name of this lady. But she remembered every word the lady spoke to her as if it was God Himself ministering to her. She stood firm and stayed in the rehab for 30 days and sobered up.

She was able to pray again and no longer angry with God but grateful that He loved her enough to send an angel to rescue her. Word got out to the public that Cynthia was in rehab for an alcohol addiction. The gospel community immediately began to slander her name.

The slandering of Cynthia's name and the people in the churches and social media dogging her image and reputation made it even harder for Cynthia to overcome her addiction. This type of treatment was mentally tearing her apart and made her depressed.

One day another gospel icon reached out to Cynthia on social media with a very loving and supportive message. And then others began to reach out to support her as well. With the love and newfound support of some friends in the industry, Cynthia slowly began to sing again and eventually she became free enough to share her testimony. She fired her original team of people.

Cynthia bore a deep hurt. She had been used by people that she trusted and looked up to. This changed how she ministered this next time around. It was much different than before. She shares how blessed she is that God is God, and when she was angry with God, he still loved her, and she had the opportunity to recover and live her life. She admits it was the people who hurt her, not God.

The problem she openly expresses is that these people claim to love the same God, but the true meaning of how God requires us to love others was not present in their lives or actions. This revelation was more evident to her than ever before. She weeps as she ministers with her music because during her brokenness, she experienced the Agape love that God has for her, and the mean spirit of those who call themselves Christians. Simultaneously.

Cynthia no longer uses addictions to cope with her reality. Instead, she does self-care regimens. Although she is aware of how certain people can be, she is also aware that she can only be responsible for her own actions and reactions. She has chosen to no longer be reckless and to respond in a mature and healthy way that is beneficial to her and her children. This is such wealth through growth.

As a result, Cynthia's ministry has grown larger than it was before.

Hiccups and falls will come in life. It is imperative that you know how to handle the fall so you can get back up on your feet and continue moving forward. No one climbs to mountain tops without trips, bumps, bruises, and gut-wrenching falls. The famous people, (and many not so famous), that you know of, that have great ministries, businesses, and careers, have this at the high price of making mistakes and being ridiculed publicly for it but persevering despite. Many have failed at attempts to do what they felt was the right thing to do and was knocked down by other people because of it, they have experienced being at the bottom with doors shutting in their face but moving forward anyhow. Many of them have lost possessions and even families, but through the Grace of God and a strength that only God can give, they got back up and regrouped, pressing forward, and ignoring the nay sayers. This is why they say only the strong survive. You must have this kind of almost supernatural strength to get up after a horrific knock down whether you caused the knock down or someone else caused you to fall. Either way, you must have the will to survive the fall and get up.

If you don't know how to cope, you won't get up from your fall to continue the climb up the mountain top. Instead, you will get up, go back down the mountain, and forget about the climb altogether. Thus, aborting the mission assigned to you by God. You will never reach the top of a mountain if you can't handle the bumps and bruises of the climb.

So many of our triumphs are born out of great pain. Just to walk in our

Divine destiny we will hit rock bottom repeatedly. Holding on to our sanity as we struggle to continue to climb. All because we realize that God said for us to do so.

You need to learn and know some coping skills for your journey. You need to equip yourself for this tedious journey so you can get up when you fall and continue to press towards the mark and make it to the top of your mountain. If you don't know how to handle adversity when it hits, you will not be mentally strong enough to continue forward and carry out the mission God has created you to complete. The whole bigger picture that God has ordained you to do this very thing you are to do is, "for the perfecting of the saints, for the work of the ministry, for the edifying of the body of Christ". In other words, to help others along their journey, like someone else helped you.

30

CHAPTER 30

THE BETRAYER

Both Havier and Cynthia were allowed by God to minister in a sin sick state for a good while. Many in Havier's circle knew he was having an adulterous affair and said nothing until one person broke the silence. Many in Cynthia's circle encouraged her to hide her alcohol addiction until one person told her the truth and asked her to get help.

When someone is in your circle and they do not tell you the truth about what you are doing, they are not your true friends. Only an enemy will sit back and watch you fall when instead they should have helped prevent the fall. The very reason a so-called friend and/or loved one will watch you gloat in your sin sick state and say nothing is because they are benefiting from it in some way. This benefit could be a monetary benefit or a social status benefit. There are many ways one can benefit from watching you silently suffer in your sin sick state. Even if that benefit is because they are jealous and want to see you fall, it's still a benefit to them.

One of the worst things we can do is to allow people, spiritual ministers, and leaders, to carry out their ministry in a sin sick mental state of mind. We are doing a disservice to everyone involved and those that need the healing that this minister is equipped to give.

When money is the motivation, and when the need for power and status is the motivation, those that will benefit will also allow and encourage the sin sick to continue to minister and hide by ignoring the present demonic illness.

In the long run, the minister gives up on their calling. They began to deny their very purpose for being created. They turn their back on God because those around them, that claimed to love and support them, encouraged the sin sick state by allowing the person to continue in silence. Then when the secret is out, the same people slander and ridicule them, kicking them when they are down. Who can believe they are useful when they are downtrodden?

This individual is now feeling devalued and sensing the selfishness of others at their own expense. When they should be feeling true love, and real concern from those that claim to love them. They should be told the truth about their condition and the harm it is causing them and others in their lives. Help should be offered to them and guidance and comfort without judgement as they travel the pathway to healing. Not left desolate to find their own way alone. Not shunned and ridiculed but lifted and cared for. Unfortunately to find this necessity is rare.

People hide skeletons in their closet and present themselves to others as though they are close to perfect while watching someone else suffer in silence. If we would just share our truths, and share our stories, more people would be healed sooner. But we don't love like we should. We don't love with a Godly love. It's a selfish, cruel, and self-centered act to encourage the sin sick individual to continue to minister and hide the sin. And then once that sickly person is outed and too low to continue to perform, we cast them aside and step on them further. Let me ask you, if you step on a ladybug and smash it with the bottom of your shoe, can it get up and survive?

Have you heard someone say, "I can't tell you the truth because you can't handle the truth"? That's a lie. A true friend will always tell you the truth. They don't tell you the truth for their own selfish reasons and that is a true betrayal of the trust that a friendship should have. Remember, these types of people are not your friends at all.

If I ask you if I look fat, and you know I look fat but tell me I look good and you like my size instead, that's lying to me. That's a betrayal of my trust all because you don't want to argue, or you are afraid I will take your telling me the truth negatively out on you. Which is not what is going to happen at all. If you tell me the truth in a loving way, it will bring awareness to the fact that I need to have a healthy diet and regular exercise plan because my being too fat is unhealthy. With the truth I will know I need to make some necessary changes and corrections.

31

CHAPTER 31

THE RESCUER

The God we serve will always send a rescuer to our aid. He doesn't just leave us out there to suffer and drown in our sinful nature. He saves us from ourselves.

We beat ourselves up with feelings of unworthiness and continue in our sinful nature. But God, sends a hand to bring us out of our self-inflictions. The sad thing is most times we don't take the hand that is being extended to help us. But God, who doesn't give up on us, will send another and another, until we finally realize we need to come out of this desolate trap. We are not one of those people who never comes back, because we understand that we must accomplish our mission, and we can't do it from a low place.

Havier's friend came and spent hours with him and invited him to the event that changed Havier's current state to that of a rescued one. A stranger came from hours away to talk with Cynthia and convince her to get the help she needed to overcome her addiction.

The rescuer is normally someone you least expect. A lot of times help is offered to us, and we refuse that help. God Himself will send someone to our rescue and we will turn them down. They will be equipped with everything that we need to get back on our feet and we will continue to waddle in the sin that we are partaking of instead. Satan makes the temptation so irresistible. So hard to walk away from. We began to feel that entertaining that sin feels better than living a Godly lifestyle and pressing towards our Divine Destiny. And we will turn the rescuer away.

The result is usually devastating. Marriages end up in divorce so often because one refuses to come out of a sinful place and work on saving the relationship with their spouse. It can be addictions, pornography, adultery, stubbornness, yes, I said stubbornness! Think about how many ways stubbornness can end a marriage. The simple act of being too stubborn to work on your marriage wholeheartedly is one way. I do not agree with the notion of getting married and as soon as opposition hits you are ready to jump out of it. You must learn to stay in there and get through things together. The divorce rate is terribly high and the two can accomplish so much more in life together. Each trial brings about a new strength to that relationship once it is overcome. Please do get effective marriage counseling and hang in there. In this case, it's the rescuer.

Often, the rescuer is simply one that has fallen prey of the same or similar devices you are currently experiencing. That person that God sends to help and aid you when you are having struggles and problems, has been where you are and overcame. That's how they are equipped to help you get out and back up on your feet. They have been there and done that.

The longer we stay in the way of ourselves, the longer it will take to reach our purpose in this life. When the Good Lord sends your rescuer, do not turn them away. Accept the help so you can get back on the right track.

32

CHAPTER 32

THE OVERCOMER

You who are no longer in a dark, dry place, are the overcomer. Havier and Cynthia are overcomers. When you have picked yourself up, done the work to heal, because that's what successful leaders do, don't walk around with sorrow or shame on your sleeve. Walk around like the warrior that you are. Praising God without ceasing because you know He brought you through.

If you choose to take on a wounded spirit, people will see you as such, and you instantly lose your position to fulfill your destiny. Because your destiny includes testimony. You cannot have a testimony if you are walking around wounded or defeated. Testimonies are of how you have overcome.

Overcomers are actively fulfilling their Divine Destiny and walking in a spirit of life and peace. If you choose not to overcome and stay stuck in your sinful nature, you lose the desire to do what you were created to do. That is a spirit of death.

The overcomer fell because someone who is in a fallen state needs to hear the truth from the overcomer's mouth of how to overcome. That's real love. Real ministry. The testimony of the overcomer is even greater than the spiritual gifting and talent. The talent is but the door opener for the overcomer to reach the audience that needs to hear the story and its truths and to see firsthand the evidence of one who fell and got up whole and restored through the Grace of God. The wealth in this right here is immeasurable. This is truly rich! The overcomer who uses his talents to share his testimony reaps blessings stored up on Earth as well as in Heavenly places.

Therefore, Overcomer, when you are in the presence of a living soul that is in a state of brokenness and\or their relationship with God is suffering a disconnect, you who are in right standing in your relationship with the Heavenly Father has an obligation to help rescue the lost one. Much like the airplane passenger that sits at the emergency exits. You are expected to diligently carry out this duty. You start by praying with them. God answers prayers. God sends you to the rescue.

The overcomer becomes the rescuer by law of attraction. When you are in a sin sick state, you attract and are attracted to other people who are also involved in what that sin is. This leads to a process of a downward spiral until you develop the strength to heal and turn completely away from that sin sick place in which you were. Once you have achieved total and complete healing coupled with faith and the necessary growth, you are now an overcomer. You can then and only then rescue others that are still in the same dungeon, that once confined even you, and you can help them in their healing and overcoming journey.

In either state, sin sick or overcomer, you will attract people who are traveling down the same or similar path as you. Depending on where you are in your process will determine how you relate to those people. Either you are going to join them, or you will rescue them.

This is a three-step process.

Step 1 includes those who are used in aiding the dark forces of this world to destroy your life. The Betrayers who are fine with you living in your sinful nature and encouraging you to continue to do so.

Step 2 includes those sent to rescue you and help you through your healing process. These people understand where you are and have experiences and testimonies to share with you for your deliverance because they were once there.

Step 3 includes you, who is now the overcomer, and those sent to you by Divine intervention to rescue and help aid them through their healing process. Starting with your prayers and testimony of how you overcame being in that very same place.

This is the order. Don't be the person who never makes it out of step 1.

33

CHAPTER 33

TIPS TO ACHIEVING YOUR GOAL

Get you a vision and achieve those goals! Did you know the Bible says that people without a vision will perish? To perish means to die. (And don't listen to Satan when he says to you, "you will not surely die"). The Bible says you will die.

If you have no direction or idea of what your purpose on this Earth is, you will just go about life, living day to day as you please. No dreams, no goals, just working a job, going home to eat and shower. Day in and day out. Not fulfilling your Divine wealth building purpose or caring to do so. If God created you with a purpose, and you are not fulfilling that purpose, what good are you to the Kingdom of Heaven? None. Sounds like perishing to me. If you buy a lawn mower to cut the grass but the lawn mower won't cut the grass, what's the use of keeping the lawn mower? You will throw the broke lawn mower out and you will get a lawn mower that will cut the grass as it is purposed to do.

Perishing in this way is a slow and painful process. Some people have ailments that require them to live with pain, until they die. That's what living without a vision is like. Living life without a purpose, walking blindly throughout life, taking the bumps and bruises as they come, until you are no longer here.

By failing to have a vision, you are stripping yourself of every possible blessing, relationship, and opportunity God has planned for you. When you are working towards manifesting your vision God opens doors for you that no man can open. These are blessings from the Lord. The people you meet along your vision journey, the blessings bestowed upon you during your vision journey, and all the wonderful opportunities that you encounter just because you are walking in your vision are there for you. None of these doors will be opened to you if you have no vision.

Write your vision and make it plain. Your vision will manifest in its appointed time. It may seem to take longer than you expected, but don't give up. Continue to work towards achieving your vision and when it comes into fruition, it will be right on time!

I did a whole vision board. I totally skipped writing it on paper and crafted up a whole large poster board with my vision on it in February 2013. I am still working towards manifesting my goals and vision on my vision board. I understand that when it does come into fruition it will be an awesome accomplishment. I will just continue to press towards that mark, and I encourage you to do the same. You can use paper or a notebook. I was just being extra!

Bottom line is, through the power of the Holy Spirit that is working within you, you will know what your vision is, and you must write it down. Then work towards accomplishing that vision with the guidance of the Holy Spirit. If you don't write it, chances are you will not follow through with your vision and the result is you will perish. You become disconnected to the Holy Spirit because you are not doing His will for your life and obviously entertaining other things. God is not a God of confusion; His Word is clear and precise. His Spirit cannot dwell in dark places, and disobedience to the will of God is a dark place. Once you are at that point of going in the opposite direction of where God has for you to go, you will be nothing but a walking corpse because the spirit of God does not inhibit those who do not serve Him. That's the death you will have. Jesus said he came that you might have life and have it more abundantly. Those who are void of His spirit, and those who choose not to follow the will of the Father, are the walking dead.

If you feel you do not know what your purpose is, I suggest you fast and pray to find out. Not knowing is not an excuse because you know that you were created with a purpose. Some people have small purposes made just for them and other people have larger purposes made just for them. It can be the same talent, just on a different scale. In many cases, people's career choices are their purpose for their life. If you are walking in your Divine purpose, you will have a Divine peace with what you are doing. When it's time to make a shift, you will become uncomfortable with what you are doing at that time and find your way into what your next calling will be. Or maybe another calling will be added to the one you are currently doing. Everyone is not limited to a certain amount of giftings and callings. The Bible tells us the Holy Spirit distributes the gifts individually as He wills. I wish I could play the saxophone or the piano as my gifts. But God didn't give me either of those talents. I am horrible at both. It would be a waste of my time, money, and efforts to try to develop either of those talents knowing neither is God's purpose for my life.

There are times when you are doing exactly what you are created to do, and it doesn't seem to be paying off and you feel like giving up. Some people do give up right at the time of their breakthrough because that's when it seems you are at your lowest point. But if you hang in there and trust that God's promise to you is true, your breakthrough will come, and you will reap bountifully. There are so many testimonies to this very fact.

34

CHAPTER 34

STOP THE FOOLISHNESS

People love to party and have fun! They are quick to tell you that you only live once so they will just enjoy partying while they are still breathing! These are not wise people at all. Just wasting money and achieving absolutely nothing in life that will equate to true wealth. In fact, they are blowing wealth on alcohol, tobacco, marijuana, food, entertainment, and the likes thereof. Money that could have gone towards building greater wealth. This is not being a good steward of what God has blessed you with. He surely will not replenish the wealth of the foolish. Please do not waste your time on throwing away money on foolish simple pleasures of this world. It is surely not wise and is a trap to keep you from obtaining wealth by enticing you to throw it away instead.

Electronics have taken over the world. People are glued to their cell phones. Everything imaginable is on the cell phone. Then we still have TV and computers. Watching TV is a favorite past time and electronic babysitter. Society is teaching kids to watch TV and stay glued to tablets and cell phones while playing games. Games? Did someone say games? Yes, I did. Video games have grown men seated for hours on end. Nowhere in all of this do we see wealth building and goal achieving. I suggest you turn off those cell phones during business hours. Limit TV and video game playing time so you can work on achieving your goals, dreams, and aspirations instead.

35

CHAPTER 35

JUST SOME ADVICE

When it's time to do tasks of any kind, it is always best to give your all. Whether it is household chores or a community project, your very best effort and skills should always be applied. This type of attitude helps build character. You will adopt this approach with everything you do in life and others will be able to trust your ability to be reliable. People do watch and pay attention to our actions and how we do things. You want to be a person that can be trusted and relied on for accountability. If you are slow to do things, messy with things you do, or even not presenting a well-done completed project, it looks bad on your character. If you know you aren't good at doing a particular skill it is better to not do it than to do it and it is not done well.

No one in this world knows everything, but we all do have different levels of intelligence and life experiences. Some people learn from life experiences and others don't. Sometimes people may have to repeat the same trial a few times before actually learning from it. The best thing to do in life is to always seek to surround yourself with someone who has more knowledge than you. This will help you grow and may help you avoid some bumps and bruises along the way because they can give you advice on how to avoid some foreseen hardships. If you are the smartest in your clique it will stagnant you and prevent growth because you have no one to learn from. Life is about learning. Learning promotes growth. Growth leads to success. Success builds wealth.

Always remember that there is someone that knows more than you. It is even a mistake to feel that you know so much that you will not listen to what others try to communicate to you. God chooses to speak to us in many ways. Often, we tune out what He is saying because of who He is using as a messenger. We miss so much this way. Give others a chance to speak to you and allow yourself to humbly review the message to see if you can learn from anything being said, regardless of the messenger. If the message is in love, it is no harm to listen and evaluate what is being said. This will earn you the respect of others and will keep you humble and growing.

36

CHAPTER 36

STUBBORNNESS

Stubbornness is big. Stubbornness is a HUGE problem within our society. Stubbornness breaks up marriages, causes people to lose jobs, and even lands some people in jail. When we are being stubborn, we are not doing the will of God. This separates us from the Holy Spirit because we are not applying the Word of God to our life when we are being stubborn. I have found that being stubborn has great consequences. The demonic spirit of stubbornness causes us to do things we shouldn't do and act in ways that are detrimental to us and others around us. It blocks us from making Godly decisions that are obviously in our best interest. Even when we know the decision we are making in stubbornness is wrong, the spirit of stubbornness prevents us from correcting our stubborn behaviors. Then we suffer in some way. Stubbornness is the trick of the enemy.

Too many times we think we know the answer to everything. We don't pray and wait for God to direct us. We make decisions on our own, thinking it is what is right for our lives when in fact it is not at all the correct decision to make. We bring unnecessary hardships upon ourselves this way. If we would simply just follow the advice and guidance of the Bible, we would make correct decisions. Of course, this requires us to read and study the Bible, which few people do. In our day and time, it is a lot of Biblical teaching on internet sites and it's not hard to find answers to make mature appropriate decisions to confirm what the Holy Spirit has already directed you to do. It's a shame to say but the truth is many times we know God's will for us and because we are uncomfortable with doing His will, we choose to do what we want to do instead. We will even convince ourselves and others that the wrong decision we are making is the right one to make. Opening the door for heartache as a result.

An example of this is people who are tit for tat. The Bible clearly tells us not to repay or try to be revengeful. But many people will still repay and try to justify it by saying, "I was just doing to you what you did to me". This type of behavior is not mature, not wise, and not Godly. It comes with attached hardships because you will reap what you have sown. If you know something is against the will of God just don't do it. Set aside your pride, stubbornness, and revengeful ways so that you can reap a good harvest.

Instead of being known for a character of stubbornness, be known for a person that is reliable and trustworthy. Do things that are right in the sight of God, so you do not hinder your blessings. Once people know you are reliable and can be trusted, it opens so many doors that you need to be open to progress towards your goals, your dreams, and your aspirations. Spiritual and natural doors remain shut for those who are spiteful and stubborn, until that characteristic is changed for the better. Some never change, don't let that be you.

37

CHAPTER 37

SERVING OTHERS

A wise way to serve others is by using your gifts and talents to do so. You can make your gift and talent into your own business and how you serve. It's important because you must serve. Others see your kindness and the Holy Spirit working through you when you serve. Jesus Christ came to serve, not to be served and that's the pattern we need to adopt because the more we give of ourselves the more we receive blessings from above.

It's wrong to think that as the leader, supervisor, president, head of any organization, marriage, or institution, that others should serve you. The correct attitude is to understand the higher on the totem pole you are, the more of a servant you should become. This way of living will create wealth. Whatever your gift and talent is, use that for your business. Businesses are also services that serve. Whatever the purpose or nature of the business may be, it is to offer a service for a fee. Since it is your gift or talent it should be something that you can lead and do well.

Take that same gift or talent and use it to serve in a charitable way as well. Charitable means without a fee. For example, if you are a nurse maybe you have your own home health business or can start a business somewhere along those lines. Also, offer your nursing skills as a nurse for the church during services and gatherings. Maybe you are a truck driver and can start your own trucking company. You can also drive the church bus or volunteer to drive for youth organizations that need drivers. I think you get the picture. Build and create wealth by serving others using your gifts and talents. By starting your own business, you will create wealth, and you will reap a harvest from your volunteer and charitable work while using the same gift and talent. It pays both ways.

38

CHAPTER 38

ROLLING WITH THE TIMES

The world is always changing. My suggestion is to roll with the changes. Otherwise, you will be left behind.

Most people are afraid of change. They are comfortable with the way things are as they know them to be. As soon as some type of change, pandemic, and/or recession is introduced to the world, some people become afraid and panic sets in.

Chosen believers should not have this reaction. The Chosen should see the evolving of the world as an opportunity to create and embrace the changes. Change with the change.

Change is not a time for alarm or panic. Each generation experiences some type of world change that creates panic upon the people. There are always the select few who do not participate in the chaos, remain calm, and create an avenue for purpose within the change.

Change is coming soon. With artificial intelligence the world as we know it is changing quickly. AI is taking over jobs that were filled by humans. Robots are being used by different government sectors to replace human manpower.

Jobs that people previously went to college and needed a degree to do them, are now being replaced with AI and robots.

Another change is services are moving over to being subscription based. Which means, you don't have ownership of those services you subscribe to, and your access can be terminated or banned by the owners at any time for any reason.

I suggest our children learn trades in school that AI cannot take over. Such careers include Cosmetology, Counseling and Therapy, Artists, Musicians and Performers, Engineers, Analysts, the Medical Industry, Fitness and Wellness, Coaches, Clergy positions, Landscaping Architects, Interior Designers, Game Wardens, etc.

Once they go to college, they need to major in subjects that AI cannot replace. Medical and judicial fields will need manpower.

Create streams of passive income that will not be affected by a recession or pandemic. This is where using your talent to create wealth comes into play.

PART 3

BEING A GOOD STEWARD OF YOUR BLESSINGS

39

CHAPTER 39

MLM AND OTHER BUSINESSES

MLM is a multilevel marketing business. It has been my experience that the people that participate in MLM businesses make a profit by getting others to join. It is usually a startup fee and then a monthly fee to remain in the MLM business. I am guilty of taking part in several over the years.

I was not profitable in any MLM business that I participated in. I lost money in each one that I invested in. God did not instruct me to take part in any MLM, I was drawn in by the sells pitch of the person that coerced me to join. Some were friends, others were family members. Every MLM I invested in was a waste. I would go to conferences and listen to the top money makers give their wonderful spill and get pumped up, yet I never saw a flow of residual income from any of them I tried.

What I learned from this and I'm sharing with you is, if it is not God's plan for you to participate in a MLM business, then it is another distraction and waste of money. We want to be good stewards of the money that we are blessed with. By us showing we have good to excellent money management skills we are then able to be blessed with increase.

In the parable of the talents the lord said to the servant who was a good steward of the talents he was given, "...well done, thou good and faithful servant: thou hast been faithful over a few things, I will make thee ruler over many things: enter thou into the joy of the lord."

It is best to be careful with getting involved in MLM businesses. Even avoiding them may be necessary unless God has directly instructed you to invest in them. If it is God ordained, you will see a steady increase monetarily and reap the blessing. Otherwise, you will be throwing away what you have been blessed with and that is not being a good steward of our blessings at all.

We want to "enter into the joy of the Lord" by having an abundance of wealth. When we are struggling financially it is very frustrating. Wondering how we will make ends meet and pay the bills. Many people experience living without electricity or running water because they didn't have the means to pay the bills. That has got to be a very humiliating feeling, which brings about feelings and actions of anger. But when we manage our money correctly, and live within our means, we can live a joyous life and give praises with ease and with a smile on our faces.

You should not look at your pay or monies coming in as a payoff for your own efforts or work. You need to understand and know without a doubt that your paycheck and monetary gains and increases are a direct blessing from the Lord. "Praise God from Whom ALL blessings flow", not some, but ALL.

40

CHAPTER 40

READING THE WORD

All Scripture is given by the inspiration of God, and is profitable for doctrine, for reproof, for correction, for instruction in righteousness, that the man of God may be complete, thoroughly equipped for every good work. 2Timothy 3:16-17.

The Bible should be read and studied in its entirety repeatedly. As you read and study the Word you can get new enlightenment each time you read the same thing you have read and studied before! It's amazing how this happens. I have no explanation for it other than its another mystery of God.

Profitable for Doctrine

The core meaning for the word "doctrine" is teaching. The Bible is profitable, (beneficial, useful, helpful), for teaching us all that we need to know. Everything we need to know about life is in the Bible. The Bible is packed with so much wisdom and knowledge that if we follow it, we will achieve the greatest height for success ever intended for our lives. Few people ever reach that status. We also need to know what the Bible says to teach others. You can't teach about something you don't know. Someone may be struggling in a certain area, and you may need a scripture or a Biblical passage to share with them how to overcome that struggle. You must know where to go in the Bible to share the needed scripture. You also must understand that scripture to convey and teach it effectively or even to apply it to your own life effectively.

Profitable for Reproof and Correction

The prudent and the wise love reproof. The fool despises it. The Bible says he that hates reproof will die! Reproof is criticism or blame. Being criticized and blamed for something is always unpleasant. But when the blame or criticism is the truth, it should be received as a positive thing. You can then accept what is being told to you and change yourself in that area for the better. That is correction. You know what it is that you are doing wrong and now the Bible is telling you how to do it the correct way. Instead of doing it your way. God's way is the correct way to live our lives. Our way is not the correct way, because then it becomes disobedience to what the Bible is instructing us to do. There are consequences for disobedience. Suffering through consequences holds us up from achieving our goals. It's best to accept the conviction of the Holy Spirit about what you are doing wrong or accept the reproof of a spiritual elder or teacher, and get yourself back on track, then to continue in disobedience doing what you want to do. It's detrimental to your spiritual growth to do so.

Profitable for the Instruction of Righteousness

As Christians we should want to live a righteous life. How we live our life is our testimony to share with others the goodness of God and the rewards that come along with living a righteous lifestyle. The entire Bible is instructions on how to live our life. What to do and what not to do. It's not many people who live a righteous lifestyle because they don't know what the Bible says pertaining to the way they are living their lives.

We are human and not perfect, yes, but the Bible also teaches us on forgiveness and repentance. Living a life of righteousness does not mean you are perfect; it means you live according to the Word of God which allows Grace for mistakes and wrong actions. Just as God extends Grace to us, those living a righteous lifestyle should understand that they must extend Grace and forgiveness to others as well. Living a righteous life is living a blessed life, because we are rewarded for doing what is right in the eyes of God.

We must read and know the Word of God to be equipped and complete. We make mistakes when our lives are filled with flaws. The Bible teaches and shows us what areas of our lives we need to work on for improvement and change. We can't get to higher heights being stuck in our fleshly ways. Not knowing the Bible will have us stuck in a lot of areas as Christians. Areas we are stuck in we can't be blessed in. We will be blessed for the good work that we do. We are not going to be blessed in our mess.

41

CHAPTER 41

SERVING OTHERS AS A LEADER

It sounds backwards, but true leaders are servants. If the leader is not a servant, he is controlling others instead of leading them.

A choir director is the leader of the choir in most cases. He is serving God with his God given talents and he is serving the members of the choir by teaching them songs to sing, how to sing them, and when to sing them. He is serving in the position of a leader.

After you have mastered your craft or talent, teach it to others. Tithe your time and talents by using them for the edification of Christ. This will open doors for you to excel in that area and you will receive back what you are putting out. Whenever you are serving someone else you will be blessed for that sacrifice.

Tithing All Three

Speaking of tithing, you must tithe your time and talents, you also need to tithe your treasure. It's important to give. When you give, you get back. What you give, meaning the type of energy you put out, is the type of energy you get back. Sow good seeds so you will reap good seeds in return.

Remember we are talking about becoming a wealthy believer, *you must do things that return good to you.* That's a wealth building key.

Putting out negative energy, like being revengeful, lacking compassion, doing mean things spitefully, etc. Will return to you what you are putting out. That is draining and takes away from the wealth you could be building by doing the opposite. Show love, show compassion, give to others, and do not take from people, be forgiving to those who have hurt you in some way, and that is what you will receive in return.

You will also be rewarded for giving your time, using your talents, and giving your monetary gains to others. When you give to nonprofits and charities you can write that off on your taxes. That is also a reward for your giving. Most churches are nonprofit organizations. Many successful people always tithe at least 10% of their earnings, they give certain charities and events their free time by using their talent. Tithing is sowing a seed, and it will reap a harvest.

There is Power in "No"

In a lot of cases, it is hard for us to say "no". We may not want to hurt someone's feelings, or we may want to do a particular activity that will interfere with our schedule to work on reaching a goal. When "no" is what is necessary in both situations.

Saying "no" when needed always has positive benefits. It also sets boundaries for us when they could be crossed otherwise.

Saying "no" protects us from the wrong thing happening in our life. Even when you say "no" to something you want to do, but realize it's not the right thing to do, you feel powerful for making the right sacrifice. Saying "no" can keep us out of trouble.

There are plenty of times you even need to tell **yourself** "No". "No" to unhealthy thoughts. "No" to unhealthy actions. "No" to unhealthy choices. "No" to going against the will of God for your life. You grow in confidence and self-discipline when you can say "no" wisely.

Nothing or no one should have control over your life but you and when you cannot say "no" to someone or something, it has control over you. When you have the confidence to say "no" to yourself and to others, you are demonstrating power.

Don't be a push over, don't give in to things you don't want to be involved in. Say "no" and demonstrate your power by meaning that "no" when you say it.

Overcoming Bad Habits and Addictions

I think it is safe to say, a lot of bad habits and addictions stem from our past experiences. Our past is a part of us. We may not be hurt as much from harmful events in our past, but we don't forget those harmful events. To cope with those feelings of rage, anger, hurt, and harmful memories of unfortunate experiences, often we develop bad habits and addictions.

No where in the Bible does it tell us to terminate our past or how to terminate our past. We just don't have a "sea of forgetfulness" within in our human makeup. Mostly the Bible tells us what to do in our future.

The whole reasoning for this is because God has forgiven us for our past. Jesus Christ died on the cross for every sin we committed, so that through Grace we can be forgiven and saved from the fiery gates of hell. Once you give your life to Christ, your past has been forgiven. This is the Grace of God.

If you are a Christian and you have sinned, then you repent, and forgiveness is yours. Then the Bible proceeds to tell you how to conduct yourself going forward with the renewal of the spirit of your thoughts and your attitude, because now you are a new person. People can and people do change.

The reason we develop bad habits and addictions is because we have not forgiven ourselves or haven't forgiven those who have harmed us in our past. Or simply because we refuse to change.

Ephesians 4:17-31 tell us how we should conduct ourselves going forward as we heal from our past, bad habits, and addictions. It reads as follows; With the Lord's authority let me say this: Live no longer as the ungodly do, for they are hopelessly confused. Their closed minds are full of darkness; they are far away from the life of God because they have shut their minds and hardened their hearts against him. They don't care anymore about right and wrong, and they have given themselves over to immoral ways. Their lives are filled with all kinds of impurity and greed.

But that isn't what you were taught when you learned about Christ. Since you have heard everything about him and have learned the truth that is in Jesus, throw off your old evil nature and your former way of life, which is rotten through and through, full of lust and deception. Instead, there must be a spiritual renewal of your thoughts and attitudes. You must display a new nature because you are a new person, created in God's likeness-righteous, holy, and true.

So put away all falsehood and "tell your neighbor the truth: because we belong to each other. And "don't sin by letting anger gain control over you." Don't let the sun go down while you are still angry, for anger gives a mighty foothold to the Devil.

If you are a thief, stop stealing. Begin using your hands for honest work, and then give generously to others in need. Don't use foul or abusive language. Let everything you say be good and helpful, so that your words will be an encouragement to those who hear them.

And do not bring sorrow to God's Holy Spirit by the way you live. Remember, he is the one who has identified you as his own, guaranteeing that you will be saved on the day of redemption.

Get rid of all bitterness, rage, anger, harsh words, and slander, as well as all types of malicious behavior. Instead, be kind to each other, tenderhearted, forgiving one another, just as God through Christ has forgiven you.

We don't want any bad habits or addictions to be an obstacle in achieving our goals or wealth building. There is a present bondage when you are bound to bad habits and addictions. We want to be free from bondage.

How do we get free from the bondage of bad habits and addictions? Ephesians tells us to "throw off your old evil nature and your former way of life, which is rotten through and through, full of lust and deception. Instead, there must be a spiritual renewal of your thoughts and attitudes. You must display a new nature because you are a new person, righteous, true, and holy."

Throw off your bad habits and your addictions by changing the way you think. That's the spiritual renewal of your thoughts and attitudes. The first step is if you haven't forgiven the offender and/or forgiven yourself, you must start there. Forgiveness is always the first step in letting go of bitterness, hurt, rage, and anger.

To let go of the negative thoughts you must change how you view them. Look for the positive lesson in the offense. Every moment of our lives is a learning moment. But if you don't pay attention to the lesson, you will never learn it. Learn what you need to learn and then change your attitude. No longer hold a grudge, or be angry, or sad. Think of the positive lesson you learned and be thankful for that lesson that you will not allow the offense to repeat itself in your life. If negative thoughts creep in, quickly remind yourself of the positive lesson, and smile because that means you won this victory! The offense can no longer hold you in bondage and the bad habits and addictions can now be cast away.

With addictions I always encourage professional help. But to go along with that, give yourself mental pictures of you not doing or needing that addiction. Think of what you can do instead. Fight the thought by rebuking it from your mind. Your own thoughts can heal and free you from the bondage of addictions. You can't doubt, you must know through faith and your determination, you can break any addiction or bad habit. Your future depends on it.

Don't forget you must now display your new nature, which is the new you. It will be obvious to others that you no longer partake in your old bad habits or addictions. Satan will try you, but you must outwardly deny yourself any chance to entertain such foolery. And be proud of the new change of freedom you have made. When you stop bad habits and end addictions, you have overcome them by breaking the chains that held you in bondage.

Don't Covet or Compare Yourself to Others

When you want something that someone else has, that is wrong to do. It seems that people wouldn't be this way, but they are. They sometimes treat the other person unpleasantly because they covet something that person has been blessed with. Some people even want someone else who is married. That is coveting because that person does not belong to you.

"Do not covet your neighbor's house. Do not covet your neighbor's wife, (or husband), Do not covet your neighbor's male servant or his female servant, (or side piece. Obviously if they willing to be a side piece it's not anyone you should want anyway), Do not covet your neighbors' animals, just do not covet anything that your neighbor owns!" Exodus 20:17

Do not covet your neighbors' cars, boats, motorcycles, ATVs, or any motorized vehicle. Do not covet your neighbor's work equipment or tools. Do not covet your neighbor's business or job. Do not covet your neighbor's success. Do not covet your neighbors' talents. Do not covet your neighbors title, degree, or position. Do not covet your neighbor's beauty. Do not covet your neighbor's spouse. Do not covet because it is the tenth commandment that God gave to Moses to tell the people. This lets you know it is a sin in the eyes of God to do so.

It is also just as wrong to compare yourself to other people and what they have that you don't. If you are focusing on wanting what another person has, you are missing the Divine purpose in their life. You are too busy looking at their material wealth or position to learn what you need to learn from them to grow and move forward yourself. Feelings of jealousy, envy, and the act of coveting are an immature characteristic. We should celebrate the success of others and see it as a testimony that we will get ours soon if we keep working hard toward what God has called us to do. If God wanted you to have it, then you would.

As far as comparing yourself to someone else, it's useless. Each one of us is uniquely made. Appreciate the beauty in others as well as yourself. I have experienced just walking around in a store and getting mean looks from other females. Either they think their man is looking at me, or they think I'm prettier, or better shaped than them, or they are bothered because at that time I had a husband by my side, and they didn't. We woman all know this is true! Women give us killer looks and It's coveting, and it's very wrong in the eyes of God. It's right up there with murder and stealing and it is equally as sinful to do.

God blesses each one of us with what we need. You're having covetous feelings of jealousy are not instrumental because all it does is put negative thoughts and low energy in the atmosphere around you. God has given to you according to what you need and can handle. If you put out this negative energy, you will most definitely get negative energy back to you. What a waste. You have dreams and goals to accomplish.

Becoming An Honest Person

When your word is good, your name is good. If anyone needs to ask about your character to someone who knows you, once they say your name and you are known as an honest person, that person will have nothing but praises and good things to say about you. Any help or assistance you need, people are willing to aid, help, and give to an honest person.

But when you are known as a liar; A person that will lie, deviate from the truth, and will make up stories, your name is mud. Your character witness will have nothing good to say about you or your words. Because your word is not good and cannot be dependent upon.

I love how the Amplified Bible says, "Lying lips are extremely disgusting and hateful to the Lord, but they who deal faithfully are His delight." Proverbs 12:22. God delights in those who are truthful.

You should not lie, or bare false witness against your neighbor, meaning ANYONE, is the ninth commandment of God. Exodus 20:16. Baring false witness includes not telling the whole story and leaving details out purposely, telling a half truth, twisting the facts, and making up your own story. Deception is not of God. The Bible says Satan is the father of lies, and fathers have children.

Jesus said, "For you are the children of your father the Devil, and you love to do the evil things he does. He was a murderer from the beginning and has always hated the truth. There is no truth in him. When he lies, it is consistent with his character, for he is a liar and the father of lies." John 9:44.

People who are liars are the children of their father the Devil, and they love to do the evil things that the Devil does. They murder the character of another, usually an up standing person of integrity and truth, with their spoken lies about the person. They are consistently lying and making up stories that are not true, just as they are led by their father, Satan, to do. Satan comes to steal, kill, and destroy, and lying on people and to people is one of his tactics to accomplish his mission.

I personally do not want to be identified as a child of the Devil. Those who lie identify themselves as such. I would like to be identified as a child of God, who is the father of Truth. And Truth will set you free. The father of lies will hold you captive and in bondage without you even realizing that is where you dwell.

Become an honest person if you are not. Rebuke that spirit of lies from your heart and your tongue. Make yourself change and only speak the truth in full. This is detrimental to where you will go in life. People who stand in truth despise liars and are reluctant to help or assist a known liar.

We Fall, But We Get Up

It's totally normal for all people of purpose to make mistakes and to have to endure a heavy blow that life throws their way. Just because you are on a Divine Mission does not mean you will be excluded from unforeseen knock downs. Just because you are on a Divine Mission does not mean you will not make costly mistakes. What makes this revelation even more devastating is that when this knock down happens, people are quick to judge and condemn, making it harder for you to bounce back.

Failure is a part of the process. The wise response to any type of knock down, those you invoked upon yourself, and those knock downs that came from others, is to learn from that failure and to get back on track.

It's hard to still show up when those you are showing up for are condemning and judging you in a negative way or entertaining the negativity being said about you. But life is still going on. You are still living and breathing and still embedded with a purpose to fulfill. You can't stay down and still accomplish your dreams and goals. It's imperative that you get up and continue towards your destiny. Ignore the judging and condemning from other people. If they are removed from your life, or not a part of your life, then it's a good thing. If they remain in your life, it needs to be because they are no longer casting negative judgement upon you. We don't need people who think and say negative things about us in our circle or have an active part in our lives. That is not an energy that is from God. It's energy from a place of darkness.

Find people who will help you get back up. God always has what we need right there for us when we need it. Don't isolate yourself during times of failure or knock downs. This is the worst thing you can do. This is exactly what I would do when I was down, I would go into isolation. While in isolation I entertained negative thoughts and stayed down and depressed. If I had allowed people who loved and cared for me to be present in those moments, I would have gotten back on track much sooner. The longer you isolate yourself, the longer it takes to bounce back.

Any opportunities or doors that closed because of your mistake or knock down is not to be of concern. Don't dwell on that. Greater opportunities will come your way once you are back on your feet and pursuing your destiny. If you entertain negative thoughts of the doors that closed on you, you will miss the doors that are now opening for you. Replace any negative thoughts of lost opportunities and relationships with positive thoughts of how you will be present for and open to even greater opportunities and more successful relationships than the ones lost.

Even when our knock downs are because of our own mistakes and doing, God doesn't stop loving us. We have a forgiving Creator who understands us and knows what we would do and encounter before it happens. Holding fast to this truth should be enough to help you get your balance and start moving towards your goal once again. You are forgiven just for asking; you are restored back to your place the moment you asked for forgiveness. It's just up to you to do what you need to do to get back to where you were prior to the fall and pressing forward once again. The blessings of God will continue in your life. You are a child of the Heavenly Father, and He loves and blesses his children always. Just do all that is necessary to get back up and continue to walk in your destiny.

Because of whom you are in Christ, anyone who wronged you will reap what they have sown. It is not your job to handle or revenge the offender. I realize from experience doing this is a hard pill to swallow. Our flesh naturally wants to get revenge on others who have done wrong to us, or to wish bad things to happen to them. But the truth of the matter is: If we stay in that negative place of revenge or revengeful thoughts, the higher powers to be that work and fight on our behalf cannot be released to avenge for us. The reason being because we are not serving or listening to anything Godly at this point. We have crossed over to serving evil instead, and we can't get up and continue our journey while in this dark place. We need to forgive our offenders, which is going to free us from playing dangerously with the demonic spirit of revenge. That spirit is a powerful evil spirit. We think the revenge we take will be justice served to the other person, when in fact it comes right back to harm us. Because what we put out is what we get back in return. So just forgive and be free from ugly dark energy and be comforted in knowing the warring angels that fight for you will now do their job and avenge on your behalf.

Save, Save, Save

1 Corinthians 16:2: On the first day of every week, (this is payday, however and whenever you get paid) each one of you, (everyone that's getting monies) **is to put aside and save**, as he may prosper, (in proportion to how much money you received) so that no collections be made when I come. (So, when financial hardships or unexpected financial costs arise, you will have savings to use for that purpose and not have to try to borrow money from someone else).

Borrowing is not a good thing to do. The Bible says we are slaves to our lender. We are to be the ones that can lend if need be. That makes us the head and not the tail. "The rich rules over the poor, and the borrower is servant to the lender." Proverbs 22:7.

I tell you the truth, it sure is hard to save when you are living paycheck to paycheck. Just barely making ends meet and every dime is needed just to survive.

I suggest starting small to get into the habit of saving if you are living paycheck to paycheck. You want to get into the habit now so when your financial situation gets better you will already be in the habit of saving and not touching the savings. If it's only $1 a paycheck. Save it, and as you begin to see an increase in what you are receiving, increase what you put into the savings.

As you continue to pursue your destiny your financial situation will get better. When you have a cushion in a savings account you feel better and less stressed about how you are going to meet your financial obligations.

Look for ways you can cut back on what monies you have going out and start placing it in a savings account. Any unnecessary subscriptions, eating out, unnecessary shopping, clubs, bars, entertainment, and sporting events, etc. Cut out or cut back drastically on things of this nature and place the money in a savings account instead.

Make grocery lists and stick to what is only on the list. Avoid ATM fees. Credit cards grow in interest so if you can keep them paid off you will save the extra interest. Find ways to cut expenses where you can and save money instead. Try to build your savings account up to include at least 3 to 6 months of what it will cost you to live monthly.

Use your talents to make extra income and remember to put in savings a portion of every dollar you make. This will also teach you to be a good steward of the monetary blessings from God and He will continue to bless you monetarily because you have shown that you can handle that type of blessing.

Time is money. When you talk to professionals for their services, such as lawyers, doctors, life coaches, even fitness trainers, you must pay for their time. People's time costs something. Your time is just as valuable. You have goals, dreams, and aspirations you are working towards. Don't waste your time.

I detest when my time is wasted because I feel as if there was something else, I could have been doing to reach my goals instead of wasting my time. I have explained this to people, and they act as though they understand, and they waste my time anyway. Whether its phone conversations, guest visiting, or even in relationships that drain or exhaust me in some way. In relationships I have always made it clear of what I expect and what I am looking to achieve, and the individual will say they agree and want the same thing and then forfeit on that understanding and I'm left to pick up the pieces, now I am off course, and must recuperate. It's not worth it, don't waste your time because you are losing money when you lose your time. Time is the one thing we can't get back; therefore, our time must be used wisely.

Deuteronomy 28

I am giving you, the Chosen believer in Christ, the keys to reach success. It is all coming from our instruction manual, the Bible. In parts of Deuteronomy Moses was giving the people of his day and our day the same keys to reach success. It is always up to the individual to apply what they have learned. Some do and some don't.

In Deuteronomy 28 it sums up blessings for those who are obedient to God's instructions and the curses of those disobedient to God's instructions. It is in our best interest to be obedient to God's instructions because that is wealth building. Wealth that will remain. The disobedient may obtain wealth, but later you hear them say, they have nothing to show for it. It didn't remain.

Let's look at Deuteronomy 28.

If you fully obey the Lord your God and carefully follow all his commands, I give you today, the Lord your God will set you high above all the nations on earth. (All you must do is apply what I am telling you in this book, obey the commands of God in the Bible, and do what the Holy Spirit leads you to do, and you will be more than good). All these blessings will come upon you and accompany you if you obey the Lord your God. (Your blessings will remain! You can show what you have done with the wealth you have received).

(As long as you are obedient) You will be blessed beyond measure, your children will be blessed, your property will be blessed, wherever you go you will be blessed.

The Lord will grant that the enemies who revolt against you will be defeated before you. They will come at you from one direction but flee from you in seven. (Remember I told you God revenges on our behalf because of who we are in Christ Jesus; because our mission is important to the Kingdom of God and if we had to fight our own enemies, we would be too exhausted and too weak to do what we were Created by God to do. Believe me, our enemies and those who do wrong to us get dealt with. The enemies will come for you, no doubt, they will come to bring you harm. But they will get dealt with in an even harsher way than how they came to you).

The Lord will bless everything you put your hands towards to do. He will give you land and bless you in the land He has given to you.

The Lord will establish you as His holy and favored child. God promises us an oath, if you keep the commands of the Lord your God and walk in his ways, then all the peoples of the earth will see that you are called by the name of the Lord, and they will fear you. (They will respect you; they will learn from you; they will listen to you; they will speak highly of you). The Lord will grant you abundant prosperity. The Lord will open the heavens, the storehouse of his bounty, to send rain on your land in season (when it's your time to reap the benefits of your harvest, it is your season), and to bless all the work of your hands. You will lend to many people but will borrow from none. The Lord will make you the head, not the tail. **If you pay attention to the commands of the Lord your God that I give you this day and carefully follow them, you will always be at the top, never at the bottom**. Do not turn from any of the commands I give you today, to the right or to the left, following other gods and serving them. (Do not let anything or anyone come before being obedient to God's Word or following through with the Divine Purpose, He has created you to do. This is always your first and main priority. When you put something or someone before what you were created to do, it or they become your god. You have abandoned your calling from the Heavenly Father, and you are no longer serving Him. You are instead serving your own selfish desires. Either God will remove that which you are serving, because He is a jealous God and you need to get yourself back to His purpose, or you will realize your mistake and do what you need to do to get yourself back to your Godly purpose. Either way, this will more than likely involve a painful process for you. It really is best to not get distracted to avoid wasted time and undue hurt and pain).

However, if you do not obey the Lord your God and do not carefully follow all his commands and decrees, I am giving you today, all these curses will come upon you and **overtake you**: You will be cursed in the city and cursed in the country. (Everywhere you go, you will not be blessed or honored. Your business will be cursed, everything you try to do will be cursed and fail, your children will be cursed and not be successful, and the land you own will be cursed). You will be cursed when you come in and cursed when you go out.

The Lord will send you curses, confusion, and rebuke, in everything you put your hand to, until you are destroyed and come to sudden ruin because of the evil you have done in forsaking Him. The Lord will plague you with diseases until he has destroyed you from the land you are entering to possess. The Lord will strike you with wasting disease, with fever and inflammation, with scorching heat and drought, with blight and mildew, which will plague you until you perish. The sky over your head will be bronze, the ground beneath you will be iron. The Lord will turn the rain of your country into dust and powder; it will come down from the skies until you are destroyed.

(And as if that isn't enough, look what else He will do!) The Lord will cause you to be defeated before your enemies. You will come at them from one direction but flee from them in seven, and you will become a thing of horror to all the kingdoms on earth. Your carcasses will be food for all the birds of the air and the beasts of the earth, and there will be no one to frighten them away. The Lord will afflict you with the boils of Egypt and with tumors, festering sores, and the itch, from which you cannot be cured. The Lord will afflict you with madness, blindness, and confusion of mind. At midday you will grope about like a blind man in the dark. You will be unsuccessful in everything you do; day after day you will be oppressed and robbed, with no one to rescue you.

(There is even more...) You will be pledged to be married to a woman (or man), but another man (or woman) will be having sexual relations with her (or him). You will build a house, but you will not live in it. You will plant a vineyard, but you will not even begin to enjoy its fruit. (In other words, you will marry and lose your spouse to someone else because of your disobedience to God. The house you two had together, you will not be living in it. Everything you put into that marriage will fail and someone else will be enjoying your wife (or husband) and someone else will live in the house that you built. The things that you invested in during your marriage union, even the knowledge the ex-spouse acquired, the gifts and material gains the ex-spouse acquired, and the positive changes the ex-spouse made, will now be enjoyed by someone else).

Everything that you own will be taken from you and given to your enemies. People that you do not know will eat what your land and labor produce, and you will have nothing but cruel oppression all your days. The sights you see will drive you mad. The Lord will afflict your knees and legs with painful boils that cannot be cured, spreading from the soles of your feet to the top of your head.

It doesn't stop there, but I'm sure you get the picture, and you can read the entire chapter for yourself. We are working towards our ambitions and our purpose here on this Earth, therefore we want to be obedient, so God doesn't curse us, but blesses us abundantly.

This message was for the Israelites, God's chosen people. These were the people God chose to be the lineage of Jesus Christ. Although this seems like God is cruel and punishing His chosen people for not serving Him, that is not at all what it means. God loves us, and He is saying there are devastating consequences for doing wrong towards others as well as devastating consequences for disobeying His Word. Those consequences can be detrimental, which is why it's best to be obedient to the Word of God.

We have become so used to people sugar coating the truth or lying about the truth entirely to spare our feelings, that it seems harsh to receive the truth when it is direct and in plain context. Instead, we interpret this directness to be harsh, mean, or a threat, when all it is, is straight forward truth that comes from a place of love.

We, who are God's chosen people, should receive the consequences of doing others wrong and disobeying God as a loving warning from our Heavenly Father. As God's chosen people, it is our responsibility to obey God's word and treat others as we would want to be treated, with love and respect added to it, and the rewarded blessings are abundant for doing so.

"For you are a holy people to the Lord your God; the Lord your God has chosen YOU to be a people for Himself, a special treasure above all the peoples on the face of the earth." Deuteronomy 7:6.

Smarter People

Surround yourself with people who are smarter than you. Do this so you can grow in your field of interest. Otherwise, if you are the most knowledgeable in your clique it will stagnate you and prevent growth.

It's good to have a mentor. Someone who is where you want to go and can guide you on how to get there. Everybody does not want to help others or provide the information to succeed. But the Holy Spirit will guide you to the right place at the right time to the right person.

Hanging out with people who are more knowledgeable than you will encourage you to step up your game. You can learn from them and strive to be where they are. They will know people you don't yet know and can introduce you to them and broaden your circle of intelligent people. They can also introduce you to new environments, such as networking events and conferences.

Being around a group of people is hard for me because I am a loner and I admittingly have social anxieties. Whatever it is that I am doing that involves some type of ministry, I must always engage with other people. I don't show the anxiety, I just prepare my mind and heart ahead of time to come out my shell and do what God has required me to do. I have performed on many stages, and I have spoken on many platforms and in my share of churches, totally nervous with my social anxieties while doing so. I continue to do ministry because doing what is required of me from God above is my number one priority. After I'm done, I will go back to my shell and get much needed rest until it's time to show my face again on whatever platform God has called me to minister on. Rest is needed from the battle within myself when I am out of my shell, as well as the spiritual warfare that takes place when I am ministering.

During the time I was writing this book, my Spiritual Father and mentor moved on to meet the Lord. I haven't found anyone yet to take his place in my life. Through the leading of the Holy Spirit, my spiritual father has placed inside my innermost being so much wisdom that I am fully equipped to move forward with confidence until God sends the next person or persons to fill the spot he had in my life. Before he became my Spiritual Father, I had no confidence at all in ministry. I didn't even speak loud enough for people to hear me in the church. Every ministry I have done has been after this awesome man of God became my Spiritual Father and mentor.

My spiritual father had so much wisdom and was so brilliant. But to look at him, I'm sure others who didn't really know him may not have thought so. He let people think what they wanted to think of him. He just operated under "thus says the Lord" and continued to be a willing vessel for the Holy Spirit to use. I am like that also, I do believe. I listen to how people talk to me, how they try to advise me as if I don't know some things, and I just let them. I don't try to outsmart them or prove to them I am smarter than they think I am. I just smile and say thank you, because they don't know who I really am and I'm okay with that. I know who I am and Whose I am.

Don't dismiss who your mentor may be because your mentor doesn't "look" like you feel your mentor should look, or have the material gains you feel your mentor should have. That's judging and you can miss out on what God has for you to learn and know. Be open to who God places in your life to mold and shape you. As you achieve new levels throughout your journey, your mentors will change and be able to equip you with what you need to continue your journey successfully.

We Serve God, Not People

Have you ever gone to a fast-food restaurant or any place of business and the person working there has an attitude as if they don't want to be there and your thoughts are, if you don't want to be here there is somebody out there who would appreciate your job!?

Do you or someone you know hate their job and complain about it all the time?

Colossians 3:23 tells us, "In all the work you are doing, work the best you can. Work as if you were doing it for the Lord, not people."

If we hold on to the attitude of gratefulness, we will understand that what we are doing is what God has called us to do at this moment, and we need to give our very best at all times with the mindset that we are not doing this job for people, but for the Lord. Whatever it is that you do or may do, use it as a platform to be cheerful and a light to all others that you encounter. Even when conditions are not quite what you like, do your very best until that job situation changes for the better.

Through the encouraging of the Holy Spirit, I know I need to be enthusiastic about the ministry that I do, because I didn't choose to do it. God chose me to do it and I must be obedient to what God tells me to do and go where God tells me to go. Doing what I have been chosen to do enthusiastically is a huge lesson for me because as I have shared with you, I have social anxieties.

Being realistic we know that not everyone likes their job, especially if it is not what God has called them to do and the door hasn't opened yet for them to walk in their calling. The big break will come one day for you to walk in your calling and enjoy what you do. Until then, serve God in what you are doing by being a light and being enthusiastic when you do it. This type of attitude will open many doors for you.

Don't Do What They Do

We can't be out here just doing what we see other people doing. We can't conform to what the world is doing. We must be transformed by training our mind to do what is good and holy in the eyes of God. We are chosen by God, and for that reason the enemies of God are going to try to get us to do ungodly things.

You must be adamant about not doing certain things and not going to certain places. Even consider what you watch on TV and what you listen to on the radio. Choose wisely who you hang out with so you can limit temptation and encouragement to do wrong.

I had a friend for many years that I truly loved. This friend had never been married and we became friends before I married. I often talked to her about my marriage and the things I was going through. I thought she was a good listener and had good advice. On a particular occasion I realized **after the fact**, that my friend had encouraged me to do something that a married woman should not do in response to my then husband mistreating me. My then husband had figured out her role in what I did, and he didn't like it. It was at that moment that I realized I had been persuaded to make the wrong choices and he held me accountable for the choices I made. The marriage was going downhill at this time, and I knew I was being mistreated. My wrong actions added fuel to an already raging fire. I do believe because my friend wasn't married, she didn't have high regards for my vows and commitment as a Godly wife in my marriage. I'm not sure she knew what she encouraged and supported me to do was wrong advice. I am sure she didn't appreciate the way I was being mistreated by my then husband, but I still should have been obedient to God and not do certain things that would be displeasing Him. A few months later I chose to distance myself from this friend. I lost my marriage and my best friend at the same time. Both by choice because neither was serving me in a healthy, Godly way. But the loss of both at the same time was very painful.

It is important to make decisions concerning separating yourself from certain people to avoid doing things against the will of God. It is wise to be strong and not give in to temptation if you haven't separated yourself from them yet. There is always a consequence to doing what is wrong, whether it is big or small. Always do an assessment of who you have around you. Are they encouraging you to only do what is right in the eyes of God?

Be careful not to get caught up in gossip, lying, slandering people's name, being selfish, being stubborn, being prideful, being arrogant, and things of the like. Those are not Godly ways nor is it the way a Child of God should conduct themselves.

Be spiritually strong and prayed up. The company you keep can lead you right to damnation.

"Do not conform to this world, but be transformed by the renewing of your mind, that you may prove what is that good and acceptable and perfect will of God." Romans 12:2.

The Message Bible says it this way, "Don't become so well-adjusted to you culture that you fit into it without even thinking. Instead, fix your attention on God. You'll be changed from the inside out. Readily recognize what he wants from you, and quickly respond to it. Unlike the culture around you, always dragging you down to its level of immaturity, God brings the best out of you, develops well-formed maturity in you." Romans 12:2.

42

CHAPTER 42

LEARN HOW TO LOVE

Please read 1Corinthians 13:4—8 and Romans 12:7-21. It is important that you truly read these scriptures before reading on.

Learning how to love is the essential ingredient to becoming a wealthy believer. Loving others in a Godly way is the core ingredient to how we are to live our lives. This is where most of us fall short and fail in general. Because we don't know how to love is why marriages fail, is why people murder or harm other people, is why people abuse and mistreat other people. It is also why people say they were hurt in the church by other Christians. Because we don't know how to love the way we are commanded to love, we fail in handling relationships in the correct manner. Because we don't love with a Godly love, we bring so much heartache amongst ourselves and others. We are commanded to love others the way Christ loves us, and we fail to learn how to do so. It's easy to say we love one another, but difficult for us to do. Majority of the time, when we are telling someone that we love them, we are lying to them and to ourselves, because if we are not loving them the way the Bible teaches us to love them, we are not correctly loving them at all.

Love does not hurt or bring pain. We as a people are always hurting others in some way or form. If someone is emotionally hurt or physically hurt by you, it's because you are not showing them love in the way you should. "Tough love" that we sometimes hear people talk about, if it isn't the type of love described in 1Corinthians 13, it isn't a Godly way to love. Not everybody is interested in living Godly. We know that for a fact. But this is for the Chosen believer in Christ, who is to live a life that is Christ like and love others in the same manner.

1Corinthians 13 tells us how to love and we ignore and don't practice loving others the way we should at all. It says that love is patient and kind. (We can be so impatient with people and so unkind towards them). Love is not jealous or boastful or proud or rude. (We can be all of those at times). Love does not demand its own way. (We are so demanding and want things our way). Love is not irritable, and it keeps no record of when it was wronged. (We get irritated easily, and always bringing up what the other person did to us). Love is never glad about injustice but rejoices whenever the truth wins out. (We will lie to get someone else in trouble or to shame their name). Love never gives up, never loses faith, is always hopeful. (We can be such pessimists. We give up on people so quickly because we don't want to truly forgive and reconcile our relationships, we don't have the faith or hope required that God can mend the relationship, and we end the relationship instead). Love endures through every circumstance. (It doesn't matter what the offense is that has been done to you, love will hold fast, and you can overcome). Love will last forever.

The hard truth is if we are going to love this way, we must be committed to living a Godly lifestyle. This type of Godly love must be learned and practiced. To love this way is against our natural nature. When we make the choice to be a child of God, many of us do not apply the instructions in the Bible of how to love others in how we live our daily lives. We are blocking our blessings when we don't love with a Godly love, and we fall short in having the testimony of how following the teachings of Christ has made a positive difference in our lives.

This is a clear example of why the worldly people say Christians are the worse kind of people. This is why unsaved people, who are hurting and who don't know Christ, don't want to come into the church and fellowship with the assembly of the saints. Many of the believers in the church do not know how to love with a Godly love.

And for those believers who do practice loving others in a Godly way, but are keeping company with those who do not, or marry someone who does not love in a Godly manner, often end up hurt. It's hard for the believer, who is extending a Godly love to another, to understand why the same grace, love, and/or forgiveness is not given back to them in return. The believer is expecting to be loved the same way they are loving the other person or treated the same way they are treating the other person in love. When this same type of love is not returned, it hurts because usually it's accompanied by anger, revenge, and unkind gestures and attitudes towards the person who is extending the Godly love. The person that is not loving in a Godly way may even prematurely terminate the relationship, leaving the other person hurt and confused, because the Godly way of loving is long suffering.

Many believers lose blessings by not loving with a Godly love as described in 1 Corinthians 13. They lose relationships and they live in unhealthy relationships, because they don't learn to love the way they should love.

This is also where the believer being unequally yoked in a relationship or marriage suffers a lot of heartache. If the believer is trying to love with a Godly love, the non-believer cannot reciprocate such a love.

1Corinthians 13 tells us what love is and the characteristics of Godly love, and Romans 12 tells us how to apply that Godly love. Starting with verse 9 it clearly says; Love must be sincere. So many times, we pretend to love others. We be polite, we speak kindly, we pretend we are interested in them, we even pretend to not like injustice done to them. When the truth is we don't care because all along it is just an act. Real love is not fake or pretense. Sincerely loving others takes sacrifice and true effort on our part. It involves helping others in some way, and it requires our time, our money, and our commitment. Committed love never leaves because it is an enduring love.

Instead of loving others in a Godly way, we become revengeful and tit for tat when an offense has taken place. Loving another in a Godly way requires us to forgive and give grace to the other person when an offense has happened. Our

Heavenly Father has extended forgiveness and grace to us when we did wrong. Grace is undeserved favor, and we are required to love the person despite the sins, just like Christ has done for us. We are not to repay evil for evil. We are not to take revenge, but to leave room for God to avenge on our behalf. We are to remain in a Godly, loving position. We overcome evil with good instead of becoming overcome with evil.

"And become useful and helpful and kind to one another, tenderhearted (compassionate, understanding, loving-hearted), forgiving one another (readily and freely), as God in Christ forgave you." Ephesians 4:32.

You must learn to love this way because it will present you as an honorable person. It doesn't make you look weak as some may perceive. Loving others with a Godly love is an admirable character quality of a strong and honorable individual.

43

CHAPTER 43

DON'T WORRY, BE REALLY HAPPY

Happiness is a choice. Most loving, kind, patient, forgiving people are happy. Believers who bear the fruit of the Spirit are loving, joyous, peaceful, patient, kind, generous, faithful, gentle, and self-controlled, are happy people. Unforgiving, jealous, angry, argumentative, and hostile people are not generally happy people.

We can all make the choice to be happy. After learning to love with a Godly love, then we must train our minds to be happy by thinking on things that are pure, honest, just, lovely, and of good report. It is not our human nature to concentrate on only these things, you must train your mind to do so to obtain happiness. You must cast down any thoughts that are not good and happy thoughts and change your thought pattern. Happiness will become your state of mind out of habitually forcing yourself to smile and think on happy thoughts. (Yes, I slipped "smile" in there!) Smile often.

Smiling releases endorphins, reduces stress, and is a natural mood booster. Smiling gives the appearance to others that you are an approachable, confident, friendly, and kind person.

The next step is to apply faith and trust in God to the equation. We can rest in happiness knowing that our Heavenly Father provides for us everything that we need and sends all our enemies fleeing from us in seven directions. We know that all things will work together for our good no matter how it may look to the natural eye. We serve a supernatural God. Our God is a miracle worker, and He is constantly working miracles in our daily lives. No need to worry about anything, God got you.

When trials and difficult times come into your life, you can rest assured that they are only a short phase of your life. You can praise your way through and still smile and be happy because you live with the promise of God that the victory is already won. Blessed people are happy people.

Miserable and unhappy people are irritated by the presence of truly happy people. They cannot understand what it is to be so happy about and doing all that smiling. It irritates them. Then they will purposely do things to try to upset you and wipe that smile off your face. These are low vibrational people. It is very unwise to match the level of these types of people. Do not match the energy that is given to you. Stay on a much higher frequency no matter how hard they try to bring you down. The truth of the matter is, emotionally and spiritually mature people do not respond negatively to low vibrational threats, comments, or actions against them.

It is very important not to let any negativity creep into your thoughts. Don't entertain any thoughts that others try to say to you that are not positive or good. Rebuke the thought and the demonic spirit attached to it. Your focus is using your talents to fulfill your purpose and goals. Negative thoughts will interfere with that. Happy and positive thoughts will keep you on the right track to your destiny.

There are so many people who will be blessed by your smile and the sunshine that you bring. Don't worry, God got it. Be happy.

Also by Vikki L. Pendleton

Other books by Vikki L. Pendleton:
KNOWLEDGE NUGGETS
BECOMING A WEALTHY BELIEVER PT. 2

Books coming soon:
BECOMING A WEALTHY BELIEVER PT.3
AFFIRMATIONS AND EXPLANATIONS
Music, Music Videos, and Social Media for

Subscribers and Fans:
WWW.YOUTUBE.COM/@DJJCHILL
IG: @dj_jchill

For Bookings:
contactjchill@gmail.com
vikki@VikkiLPendleton.com

All related websites:
FeelizePublishingHouse.com
FeelizeEntertainment.com
VikkiLPendleton.com

www.ingramcontent.com/pod-product-compliance
Lightning Source LLC
Chambersburg PA
CBHW060529130626
46553CB00002B/694